BEARD ON

James Beard had a lifelong love affair with food. His first book was published in 1930, after which he wrote nineteen books on food, including the best-selling *James Beard Cookbook* and his highly popular *Beard on Bread.* James Beard died in 1985.

BEARD ON PASTA

James Beard

Drawings by Yvonne Skargon

MACMILLAN

First published in Great Britain 1984 by Michael Joseph Limited, by
arrangement with Alfred A. Knopf Inc.
in paperback in Great Britain

First published in paperback in Great Britain 1985 by
PAPERMAC
a division of Macmillan Publishers Limited
4 Little Essex Street London WC2R 3LF
and Basingstoke

Associated companies in Auckland, Delhi, Dublin, Gaborone,
Hamburg, Harare, Hong Kong, Johannesburg, Kuala Lumpur, Lagos,
Manzini, Melbourne, Mexico City, Nairobi, New York, Singapore and
Tokyo

Typeset by Cambrian Typesetters, Aldershot

Printed in Finland

British Library Cataloguing in Publication Data

Beard, James
   Beard on pasta.
   1. Cookery (Macaroni)
   I. Title
   641.8'22   TX809.M17

ISBN 0-333-38881-X

TO BEATRICE PETERSON
a great teacher and good friend

CONTENTS

INTRODUCTION

This is a book of good times to have with pasta.

I never get tired of pasta, any more than I get tired of bread. I eat it when I'm exhausted and want a quick meal that will give me a lift. I eat it when I'm in an ambitious mood, looking for something pleasant and different to compliment a guest.

When I want something spicy, I toss spaghetti with warm olive oil, garlic and anchovies. When I want something voluptuous, I bake elbow macaroni (tubetti lunghi) in a cheese-rich béchamel sauce. And, when I'm fed up with complicated foods, I fill a bowl with piping-hot green noodles and cover them with icy tomatoes and chopped spring onions in a sharp vinaigrette.

Pasta is always the same, yet always different. It has a comforting familiarity, with its pale golden colour and chewy, wheaten taste. And then there are all those amusing shapes, and the thousands of ways to eat them with sauces: from avocado to courgette, or from plain butter and cheese to purée of frogs' legs.

It's always different because we find pasta recipes in nearly every country in the world. I should say right at the start that this isn't an Italian cookbook. It's a collection of worldwide pasta dishes that I like and like to make. There are Italian recipes in it. But there are also dishes from Germany, France, China, and Greece. There is a kosher-style noodle pudding and an English macaroni dessert.

In my own life, pasta didn't begin as an Italian food at all. I must have been six or seven before I ever ate spaghetti, but I was eating Chinese noodles long before that.

They were given to me by Let, the Chinese chef who worked for my mother. He used to make a soup that was a rather weak chicken stock absolutely full of noodles, ham, spring onions and thin strips of egg that he had beaten

9

up, cooked in a thin pancake and then sliced into strips.

We went fairly often to Chinese restaurants in Portland, and I loved the chow mein and fried noodles. It was nothing like the chow mein on beds of crisp little twigs that you get now. It was more like lo mein. The noodles were boiled and then quickly fried so that they were brown and crispy on the bottom, and they would be covered with shredded vegetables and cubes of tofu (soya bean curd).

I didn't have Italian noodles until I went to school, when we started going to a pretty good Italian restaurant that served 'family-style' meals at great long tables. They'd bring you a little antipasto and then a dish of pasta. The menu never varied, and it was always fifty cents. They made a good tomato sauce, and one with butter and fresh herbs, and a version of carbonara. The sauces were nothing complicated, but it was great fun, and I just loved it; and, after all, what can you do for fifty cents?

Oddly enough, when I began to cook pasta myself, it was in the German style. That was because my mother had close friends who were from a German family, and they used noodles a lot in soups and with stews. They had one wonderful dish for which they took all the lesser parts of the pig — the backbone and the tail and such — braised them, and served them with sauerkraut and noodles. That was fun.

The point of all these reminiscences is to show how, even in a small American city at the beginning of this century, there were several quite distinct traditions of cooking with pasta.

I don't know where the historians will eventually tell us pasta started. I'm sure, however, that the old romantic notion that Marco Polo came back to Venice from China toting the secret of spaghetti has been pretty much debunked.

My guess is that we will never find a starting place for pasta because it will turn out to have popped up in several different places, all quite independent of one another, and then to have been carried along the trade routes by camel, ship and peddlar's pack.

You just have to look at rice noodles and mung-bean or cellophane noodles to see that the Oriental tradition is quite separate from ours. Or to consider the very early Bulgarian pasta — lumps of dried dough that horsemen carried in their saddlebags and grated into pots of boiling milk at the end of the day's ride.

We do know that there is a long history around the Eastern Mediterranean of making simple wheat doughs for boiling. We know that noodles were being sold in Greece as early as the fifth century. Pasta in Italy probably started in the south, as part of that whole Mediterranean culture. We know that the Romans grew wheat in Sicily; and what better way is there to preserve wheat flour than to make it into a paste and dry it?

Yet the first Italian references to pasta are terribly offhand. A legal document mentions that someone has inherited a basket of macaroni or a sieve for draining noodles. Or a saint's legend tells how the devil was foiled in his scheme to fill a virtuous man's pasta with dirt. It seems that the saint was present at that meal. When he said the blessing over the food, the dirt was transformed into sweet Ricotta, and everyone enjoyed a good dinner. What a wonderfully Italian miracle that one was!

It's just because pasta is part of the cooking of so many different cultures that we don't have to feel bound by the rules of any one country when we cook it. That's why I've made no attempt in this book to be particularly classical or traditional. My aim here, as in all my books and teaching, is to encourage pleasure and individual taste in the way we eat.

Of course there are well-established rules in Italy about the right way to serve and eat pasta. These are customs that have grown out of centuries of experience, and they have the authority of a lot of good eating behind them.

In the question of matching pasta to sauce, for example, the Italians can be very specific. Marcella Hazan says one should use thin spaghetti for seafood sauces, regular spaghetti

11

for cream sauces. Giuliano Bugialli says you should try always to serve pesto sauce on trenette, which is a flat, narrow noodle.

But we don't have to do things the classic Italian way. We can do as we please.

When we pick a pasta to go with a sauce, we feel free to experiment and discover what appeals to us. Once we've chosen our sauce, we try to imagine how it will taste. What pasta would go well with it? Will it take a chewy ziti, delicate angel's hair, or rice-like orzo?

We may find, eventually, that certain pastas seem right with certain sauces. That tubular shapes, like penne, and envelope shapes, like sea-shells (conchiglie), seem right when a sauce has tiny bits of meat or fish to be caught in the spaces. That fine, slender noodles seem proper with thin tomato sauces. That we want a good chewy twist (fusille) to stand up to a cold pasta salad full of cheese and broccoli.

But you shouldn't take this on anyone's authority, least of all mine. Instead, consult your own taste and style, and feel free to experiment. Take chances. No one should be intimidated by other people's opinions on what one should eat.

Nor should we be intimidated in the area of table manners and propriety. Pasta is not a mannerly food to eat. I remember when American hostesses were so insecure and etiquette-conscious that they would break up noodles into inch-long pieces before they cooked them, and would choose short-cut macaroni rather than spaghetti so that their guests wouldn't risk the crime of slurping at the table.

I think most people have got over that kind of tea-room niceness, but now there is another worry people have about eating pasta, which is of not doing things in the proper Italian way. They worry about whether the Italians use bowls or plates, and whether it's proper to serve a spoon along with the fork as a help in picking up the strands, and how to avoid slurping up the last inches of long noodles.

To which I say that it's time to stop worrying and start enjoying.

Shallow bowls are nice to have and they make it easier to pick up the pasta. But, if you don't have them, then plates are fine. Remember that the Chinese hold a small bowl under their chins and shovel the noodles into their mouths with their chopsticks.

Do you serve a spoon alongside your spaghetti? Italians say that only children, the infirm and the ill-mannered use spoons as props for their forks when picking up pasta. I think spoons serve a most important function, that of getting up the sauce left at the bottom of the bowl. I've often wiped up the last flavourful puddle of oil and garlic with a crust of bread which was a good, if starchy, solution. But if you have a spoon, you can capture the last cream-covered peas and prosciutto, the last basil-flavoured tomato sauce or capers in olive oil from the bottom of the bowl.

As for picking up the pasta, use the spoon if it helps. The Italians have perfected a technique for picking up long strands on a fork. They stick the fork into the mass of pasta and twirl it around once or twice until they have a neat amount of pasta wrapped around the tines. One warning: experienced eaters are careful to start with just a few strands of pasta on their forks, or else they wind up with a package that is larger than their mouths can accommodate.

How do you deal with the short strands that are left hanging from your mouth? Without embarrassment, certainly. It's bound to happen when spaghetti is cooked just right, because only overcooked pasta is soft and pliable enough to form a tidy package around the fork. A few luscious strands are bound to hang loose, and must be taken into the mouth as skilfully as possible. If you slurp them, so be it. Because the truly best way, the only classical and true way, to eat pasta is with gusto.

OBSERVATIONS

COMMERCIAL DRIED PASTAS
(Italian and continental pasta · egg noodles ·
Chinese and Japanese dried noodles)

SHOP-BOUGHT FRESH PASTA

FLOUR FOR HOME-MADE PASTA

EQUIPMENT FOR MAKING PASTA
(mixing · rolling · shaping ·
pasta-making machines)

COOKING PASTA

PORTIONS

IMPORTANT INGREDIENTS
(tomatoes · olive oil · cheese)

WHAT TO DRINK WITH PASTA

COMMERCIAL DRIED PASTAS

ITALIAN AND CONTINENTAL PASTA

I'm a great fan of good commercial pasta made with durum wheat. It has a mellow flavour and strong texture that are standards for what good pasta should be.

The clue is in the words 'durum wheat', 'durum' or 'pura semolina'. You have to read the ingredients on the packet, and buy only pasta that is made with durum-wheat flour. (The name comes from the *Triticum durum* wheat.)

Most, although by no means all, of the Italian commercial brands are pretty good. De Cecco maintains a tremendously high quality and produces hundreds of different shapes. But I've also had Italian dried pasta that was no good at all.

Among commercial pastas, I've always found that Buitoni makes a damned good product. It's not fair, however, to name one brand, because there are usually small pasta manufacturers to be found wherever there is an Italian population. Every so often I am invited to the Macaroni Luncheon in New York City (and I go with pleasure, because you get a first-rate meal there). All the small local factory owners are introduced and asked to say a few words, and I can tell you that these introductions last throughout the whole meal. Dried Italian-type pastas are also made in Greece, Great Britain and France. Whether in London, New York or Rome, you just have to become ingredient conscious, and choose only brands made with durum-wheat flour.

Also commonly available now is whole-wheat pasta, in a variety of shapes, and I just love it. It's not only the colour but the special nearly meaty chewiness that I find appealing.

At the moment, we are in the midst of a kind of snobbery: people think that any fresh pasta is better than any dried pasta. That just isn't so. There is nothing wrong with good commercial pasta; in many cases it is better than the fresh pasta you can buy.

EGG NOODLES

Your local supermarket probably has several brands of home-style egg noodles in boxes and cellophone bags, many of them with Central European or American names. Some of them are pretty good, as long as you use them for the dishes they were designed for. Use them for noodle pudding, for pork with sauerkraut noodles, or for Alsatian chicken and noodles. You'll be disappointed if you try to use them in an Italian dish.

CHINESE AND JAPANESE DRIED NOODLES

In recent years, many small oriental food shops have opened, and these almost always stock specialities, such as udon, buckwheat, rice and mung-bean or cellophane noodles. I've found all the brands to be quite reliable, although perhaps I don't bring to them the educated palate that I do to Western pastas. Just be sure to use them properly.

Rice noodles or sticks, made from ground rice, are more fragile than wheat noodles. They need a brief soaking before you cook them. Mung-bean noodles are made from powdered mung beans. They too have to be soaked, after which they are gelatinous and springy. They don't actually need any cooking at all after their soaking, but can be briefly stir-fried, the way you do bean sprouts. Udon and buckwheat noodles act like ordinary wheat noodles. Follow the instructions given on the packets in each case.

SHOP-BOUGHT FRESH PASTA

The best fresh commercial noodles I've ever had are the ones I buy in New York's Chinatown. They are made with flour and water, and come in just a few shapes. You buy them soft, packed in plastic bags, and should store them in the refrigerator.

In large cities one can usually find several grades of fresh pasta, especially where there is a large Italian population. Many Italian shops in London's Soho district make their own spaghetti, tagliatelli, tortelloni etc.

But just because pasta is fresh doesn't guarantee that it's going to be good. There is now so-called fresh pasta that is sold in cardboard trays in supermarkets which is far inferior to good dried pasta. This is one occasion when freshness does not ensure quality. I believe it's far better to use a first-rate dried pasta made of durum-wheat flour than a trendy, mushy brand that dissolves in the water like a dumpling.

FLOUR FOR HOME-MADE PASTA

All the recipes in this book were tested with 'all-purpose' flour because that's the kind most commonly available in America (it contains some hard wheat and therefore has a certain gluten content). In most cases it is inter-changeable with British plain white flour (*not* self-raising). But it isn't the best flour for making pasta by any means. The best you can get is a hard-wheat flour, which in Britain is the flour sold as strong white bread flour. Some specialist shops also sell a special durum or pasta flour for pasta-making, but for all practical purposes, strong white bread flour, easily obtainable now, is the best to use.

All wheat flour contains a protein called gluten. It's the gluten in the wheat that gives tension and elasticity to dough. Durum-wheat flour has more gluten than ordinary flour, and it makes not only the best pasta but also the best bread. A dough made with this flour will be noticeably easier to knead and to roll out than one made with plain white flour.

Many commercial pastas are made from semolina or durum semolina, which is coarsely ground hard wheat, less fine and more granular in texture than strong wheat flour. I use it mostly for dishes such as gnocchi and spätzle and sometimes to make bread. I have made pasta with it, but don't try using it in a pasta machine — it will clog up the works.

Whatever flour you use, just remember that you can't count on it having a standard quality. It often varies with age and with the temperature in the shops and in home kitchens. That's why you may sometimes have to add a little extra oil or a tablespoonful or two of flour to get your dough to the proper consistency.

EQUIPMENT FOR MAKING PASTA

MIXING

You can get a good dough every time using either an electric mixer or a food processor. But it isn't difficult to mix by hand: it's the kneading that takes all the work. For hand mixing, you just need a good work area and a fork.

Dough scrapers are useful for cleaning off the board after you've combined the flour and eggs to make the dough.

ROLLING

If there is one piece of pasta-making equipment I wouldn't want to be without, it is my Bialetti pasta machine. It works on the principle of the wringer, squeezing the dough between two cylindrical plastic rollers until it is paper thin. I have the motor-driven machine, which makes an infernal racket but produces good pasta, and I just love it. I know people who own the hand-cranked machine and like the sense of control they get with it. The hand machine is a lot cheaper and infinitely quieter than the motor-driven machine and, as far as I can tell, one is as good as the other when it comes to rolling and cutting the dough. If you're going to spend any money on this business of making pasta, this is where you will want to do it. (Egea is a hand-cranked machine available in Britain.)

If you're rolling by hand, you should know about the special long rolling pin made for pasta. It's about 90 cm (3 ft) long, and is the same width all the way down. (My guess is that it was modelled after the broomsticks that people have used for years to roll pasta.) According to Marcella Hazan, this pin should be hung vertically for storage so that it doesn't warp. I brought one home from Italy years ago. It's thinner than the classic wooden pin — about 3.5—5 cm (1½—2 inches) in diameter — and I have trouble using it because my hands are too big.

When you roll the dough by hand, you'll need a good working area. Marble is perfect for it, but of course wood works very well, and is the traditional surface in Italy. Many people like to use a pastry cloth as a kind of security blanket against sticky dough, but I've never felt the need of one.

When you're rolling the pasta, you might want to have a big soft brush on hand for dusting it with flour, just as you would when you make puff pastry.

And, while we're talking of rolling by hand, let me say that good, strong stomach muscles are a help so that you

20

can lean your tummy against one end of the sheet of pasta while you're rolling and stretching the other end. And arm muscles, too, are helpful for dealing with a properly stiff dough!

SHAPING

You can cut out the noodles with your small pasta-making machine, simply by changing from the smooth rollers to the cutting rollers. Or you can fold up the sheets of dough and then cut them with a sharp knife. But it's helpful to have a rolling blade, straight-edged or wavy, of the sort that is used to cut out ravioli, pastry strips and pizza slices.

PASTA-MAKING MACHINES

It was inevitable that the manufacturers would copy the pasta industry and produce small machines for the home kitchen. These machines push the dough through a die so that it comes out with a shape.

There are two kinds. With the first, you still mix your dough in the traditional manner, either in the electric mixer or the food processor. Then you put it into a container from which it is pushed through shaping dies. This is the method used in Magimix and other machines, but the special attachment is not available in Britain as yet.

In the other machines, such as the Simac and Bialetti (and there may be more on the market by the time this is printed), you simply put flour and eggs in the opening at the top of the machine and, after a suitable amount of time has passed for kneading and processing, the pasta comes out the other end.

The one thing these machines give you that few people have ever had before is absolutely fresh round and tubular pasta. That's because, even in Italy, pasta that is formed by extrusion is always made in factories and sold dried.

I suppose that we have to take it for granted that these machines are going to be part of our lives, and to hope that they will at least introduce home-made pasta to people who would never dare to make it in any other way. They turn out a reliable product, and they do their job in less than five minutes.

I have a few reservations about them, nonetheless. I'm not sure that they produce as flavourful a pasta, or pasta with as good a texture as we can get by traditional methods, owing to the fact that the manufacturers recommend that you use soft-wheat or cake flour. (Soft-wheat flours have little gluten and cake flour, a silky-textured fine flour used, as might be expected, for cakes, is not generally available in Britain.) While the product looks and acts the same, you just aren't going to get the flavour from cake flour that you will get from good strong wheat flour. But strong wheat flour tends to clog the dies of the machines.

And, although the machines are time-savers in one sense, they eat up time later on. If you use a small die, it takes a great deal of time to get it spotlessly clean. You have to poke out every crumb of dried dough from the die, or it won't work properly the next time you use it. When I tried one of the machines, it took me nearly an hour to worry out all the caked-up dough left in the dies. The manufacturer had even provided a little double-edged toothpick for the job!

As I write this, we're just in the beginning of the development of the new machines. Who knows how they will be improved once thousands of pasta makers get to working with them? But at the moment my opinion is that you can't do better than to mix the dough in the mixer or food processor and then put it through a small pasta rolling machine. You'll have a beautiful pasta with superior texture and taste.

For making ravioli, I have a marked rolling pin. You roll it over a sheet of dough and it marks squares on the sheet. You put dabs of filling in the squares on half the dough, fold the other marked half over it, and then cut along the lines with a knife or rolling blade.

I've also used ravioli trays, metal trays with shallow indentations in them. You lay the dough over the tray, and drop bits of filling into the hollows. Cover them with a second sheet of dough, and run a rolling pin over it all.

You can buy round or square tortellini stamps that work like pastry or biscuit cutters. As a matter of fact, if you have a round pastry cutter, use that instead.

COOKING PASTA

Although I've been cooking pasta nearly all my life, the one thing I can't begin to tell you is how long it is going to take. The time varies too much, depending on the heat of the day, the amount of water in the pot, the kind of flour used, the proportion of flour to liquid in the dough, the shape of the noodles, and how long the pasta has sat in the warehouse and on your shelf.

All I can say is that fresh pasta cooks quickly, and that you should start testing it as soon as the water in the pot returns to the boil. Dried pasta made with plain or strong flour cooks in far less time than the instruction on its box recommends, and should be tested after 3 or 4 minutes: it can become mushy very quickly. And I've had dried durum-wheat pasta from Italy that was supposed to be done in 8 minutes, and that I had to cook for a full 15 minutes before it lost the final core of uncooked dough in the centre. I just had to keep fishing out strands with a fork and biting them until the noodles were at the point I wanted.

You start with a big panful of furiously boiling water. Your pan should be really big, holding 7—9 litres (12½—16 pt). Buy one with high sides so that it sits right over your burner.

I've seen pans that had strainers or steamers that fit right into them, so that when it was time to take out the pasta you simply lifted out the strainer and the excess water ran back into the pan. This is especially good for making lasagne, when you cook only a few strips at a time, and want to save the boiling water.

For stirring, many people like to use wooden paddles that look like flattened spoons with 2.5-cm (1-inch) wooden sticks protruding from them. They're pretty good because they don't tear the pasta, but I've always used a big fork and spoon or a set of tongs instead. The point of using wood rather than metal is that wood doesn't conduct the heat from the boiling water to your hand. There are many such pasta tongs available.

A flat skimmer, like a gigantic tea strainer, is useful for removing the first batch of wontons or kreplach from the water before you drop in the second batch.

And you'll need a big colander for draining the pasta. Be sure that you've got one that's large enough, and that it stands steadily on a circular base and not on three rickety feet. Otherwise, one day you'll pour in the pasta and boiling water and see the colander tip over and dump your pasta down the drain.

As for rinsing, I know that some books tell you to rinse the drained pasta under cold water to get rid of the starch. All that does is cool off your pasta, and I think it's a damned silly idea. Should you rinse with hot tap water? Frankly, I usually don't rinse the pasta at all, letting the volume of boiling water that pours over them from the pot carry away anything that shouldn't be there. But, if they should stick, then go ahead and rinse. Just use very hot water.

One important point: don't let the pasta sit in the colander while you prepare a sauce — even a quick sauce. Pasta should be tossed as soon as it has drained. After it's drained, the pasta should go into a heated bowl and be mixed immediately with some or all of the sauce. However, if you want the pasta or noodles to cool for a salad, then add some butter or oil and toss gently, to keep the strands from sticking together as they cool.

Sometimes it's a good idea to add the pasta to the pot that holds the simmering sauce, give it a good stir, and let it warm over a very low flame for 1 or 2 minutes while you get the warm plates for serving.

PORTIONS

The rule of thumb is that 450 g (1 lb) of pasta serves 4 to 6 people as a main course and 6 to 8 people as an appetiser. If you need a rule of thumb, that's as good as any, but it doesn't take into account the richness of the sauce, the level of formality of the meal, or the appetites of your guests.

At a trattoria in Italy you are served a great glob of pasta as a first course because they aren't going to give you a large portion of meat afterwards. But in an elegant restaurant in New York or London you may get just a heaped spoonful of angel's hair with truffles as an appetiser, just enough to awaken your palate. And what about a dish like macaroni and cheese? The meat eaters will take small helpings alongside their hamburgers. The vegetarians will serve themselves quite a lot since it is their main dish. And the dieters won't take any at all, but will pick the best chewy burnt bits off their neighbours' plates.

That's why I've been imprecise when giving the number of servings you will get from the recipes in the book, why I say that a dish will serve '4 to 6' instead of being more definite. The number of servings will depend on the place in the meal, the quality of the sauce and the appetites of the eaters.

IMPORTANT INGREDIENTS

TOMATOES

If you can buy good fresh tomatoes that are sweet and juicy and well fleshed, then you are blessed. Unfortunately, there is a terrific variation in the quality of tomatoes on the market, and most often what you get are tomatoes that taste like pink flannel and feel as though they were put up in a munitions factory. You can't judge by the look of them, either. I've often been fooled by beautifully scarlet Italian plum tomatoes that turned out to have no taste at all. In general it's always better to go for large tomatoes — called Marmande or Beefsteak — rather than the perfectly round and fairly tasteless tomatoes grown for the British market.

If you can't get wonderful fresh tomatoes, tinned tomatoes are your best bet. The large canneries buy up the pick of the crop, and they put them in tins when they are really ripe. You'll have to test a number of different brands to find the one you like best. Tinned imported plum tomatoes in juice come from Italy and various other countries. Also available in tins are chopped plum tomatoes and, occasionally, condensed tomato (partially evaporated) which is half-way between chopped tomatoes and a runny purée or paste. Try any or all of them.

But none are the same as fresh, and I'm afraid that they don't work the same. That means that the result of your cooking may well vary depending on whether you use good fresh tomatoes, bad fresh tomatoes, or good or bad tinned tomatoes. You'll have to adapt your cooking method to the kind of tomatoes you have available.

If you find that your tinned tomatoes are watery, you can either cook them down or intensify the flavour by adding tomato purée or paste. I prefer to cook them down because I think that tomato purée sometimes gives an overly sweet taste with a bitterness just behind it. But, if you do use purée, by all means look for the kind that comes in tubes. That's one of the most sensible innovations in packaging I've seen in years, allowing you not to feel conscience-stricken if you use only one tablespoonful at a time.

And, if you're lucky enough to find a grower selling slightly over-the-hill end-of-summer tomatoes, buy all he will sell you. They may not be right for slicing any more, but they'll be wonderful to peel, seed and cook with onion and garlic into a huge pot of tomato sauce. Frozen in portions of about 225 ml (8 fl oz), the sauce will brighten your kitchen all winter long.

TO PREPARE FRESH TOMATOES FOR SAUCE:
Dip tomatoes in boiling water for 30 seconds. Remove skin and cut a slice from the stem end. Squeeze tomatoes firmly to extract seeds and liquid. Chop flesh very finely.

OLIVE OIL

Olive oil comes in several grades, of which the top of the line is called 'extra-virgin olive oil'. This means oil from the first pressing of the olive, and it is very green, rich in taste, and very expensive. It is available in continental grocers. The best and fruitiest olive oil, to my mind, comes from the South of France. After that, in descending order, come oils from Italy, Greece, Spain and North Africa.

Don't store olive oil in the refrigerator, or it will thicken and turn cloudy. Instead, leave it out on the pantry shelf. When kept too long or exposed to heat, olive oil can turn rancid so it is best to buy it in small quantities if you don't use a great deal.

When the flavour of olive oil is not part of the essential taste of a dish, I often use a good cooking oil, such as peanut oil, or I mix peanut and olive oils half and half, to temper the taste of the olive so that it doesn't overwhelm the other ingredients.

CHEESE

If I had written this book twenty-five years ago, I would have limited the cheeses to Parmesan, Pecorino Romano, Cheddar, cottage, Emmenthal and Gruyère. Perhaps I would have mentioned Mozzarella, too, but I'm not sure. In that short list I would have named every cheese I could be sure was available to my readers.

Since that time, however, there has been a revolution in the kinds of cheese we enjoy and import. Our palates have become accustomed to a great many new cheese flavours. And every season brings several new names to our local cheese shops: new varieties of cheese, variations on old favourites, familiar types of cheese now being made in new locations. Twenty-five years ago, goat cheese was considered too chalky and sharp for most people. Then we learned that goats' milk is naturally low in fat. And suddenly, Chèvre is available everywhere.

Best of all, this explosion of interest has been in the realm of natural cheese. It has nothing to do with all the processed cheese and processed cheese food and imitation processed cheese food, all of which taste like rubber and all of which act in an infuriatingly unpredictable manner when you try to cook with them.

When I was testing recipes for *The New James Beard*, I saw that there had been a revolution in our eating habits and our cooking. We are going through an especially lively period in the history of cooking. Rules are being thrown off. Recipes are finally recognised as guides rather than as commandments.

I refuse to accept that any cook be bound by rules and restrictions. Your taste is your only guideline, and the more you follow your taste, the better cook you're going to be.

If there is no good melon to serve with your prosciutto, you can have it instead with figs, or with thin slices of melting-ripe pear or with fresh pineapple: whatever is freshest and appeals most to your palate.

The same freedom applies when we cook with cheese. Constantly tasting as he goes, the new cook learns to appreciate the subtle changes that occur when he uses a mild Danish blue cheese, a sharp Roquefort, a creamy Gorgonzola, or a mellow Stilton. If the tomatoes seem flavourless, he selects a strong Italian Fontina rather than a bland Mozzarella to melt over them.

The only rule is to taste as you cook, and to do it often. Never let a recipe become a rigid formula. There is no such thing as the right cheese for a particular dish. During the months when I was testing the recipes for home-made noodles for this book, I happened to have on hand a large wedge of pungent Caciocavallo, a hard, salty cheese from Italy. At the end of most testing sessions, when the fresh noodles went into the boiling water, a piece of Caciocavallo would go into the food processor at the same time, and lunch would be hot noodles, unsalted butter and tangy grated Caciocavallo. But I could just as well have used an aged Gouda or a true Parmesan on the pasta.

There are reasons beyond taste to free yourself from rigid formulas for cooking with cheese. The 'right' cheese might not be available to you. In Greenwich Village, where I live, I am surrounded by well-stocked cheese shops, and in my travels around America to teach I have seldom been in a city that doesn't have at least one — how I detest the name! — 'gourmet' shop. Food mail order is also a growing business.

Even so, not all grocers carry all kinds of cheese. Stocks fluctuate with the season and with the clientele. And I know, because of the letters I get, that there are many good cooks who have to rely on local supermarket produce and who, if they can't get real Parmesan, don't want to be forced to use those dreadful and expensive little jars or packets of pre-grated cheese. They're better off using a sharp mature Cheddar.

And then there is the matter of price. The days are long past when cheese could be considered a budget-priced protein. True Parmesan — the kind that is made near Parma and marked 'Reggiano' — is very expensive. Most people prefer to serve it for eating these days, considering it too costly to grate over a highly seasoned sauce. Instead, they will choose another grana from Italy or a Pecorino to go on their spaghetti. It's important to know that there are less expensive choices available that will in no way diminish the quality of your dish.

While we're talking about price, we should say something about left-over cheese. Many people like to offer a selection of cheese with salad or fruit at the end of the meal. One thing that destroys me is the way people cut cheese from a cheese board. If you take care of cheese, if you cut it in regular wedges or slices, you'll have less surface to dry out, and you keep the cheese looking good enough to serve a second time. But you can't stand over your guests, glaring at them if they hack off a hunk here and there, and so usually, after the cheese has been brought out two or three times, it turns into a decidedly awkward, mutilated chunk. There's no reason to throw away a piece of cheese just because there's nothing left but an unattractive end. Instead, recycle it for later cooking.

If you have a semi-soft cheese, such as an end of Brie or Fontina, slice it with a sharp knife or grate it against the large holes on your grater. If it is a hard cheese, you can dry it out further by leaving it, unwrapped, in the refrigerator for a few days. Then put it in the food processor, grate it and store it, covered, in the refrigerator or freezer. Most cheese freezes surprisingly well. The next time you need a few tablespoons of cheese to enrich a vegetable soup or a gratin, use the grated cheese.

A word about grating cheese. I like to use my food processor for the job. But Evan Jones, who knows more about cheese than anyone else I know, tells me that in his house they use an old-fashioned four-sided grater. And there are metal rotary graters which many people use, but I find those annoying because I can't put in a big enough chunk of cheese to make it worth the effort and, somehow, it doesn't fit in my hand properly. If you want the cheese to sing with flavour, try to do the grating at the last minute, just as you grind pepper at the last minute.

To give you a start, I'm going to list the kinds of cheese most often used with pasta. I've grouped them according to type so that one can be substituted for another, even though there are subtle variations in flavour. I hope that you will refer to the list before you go shopping, so that you will know what you are getting. Then, if the Gruyère doesn't look good to you, you can select a Danish Samso or some Emmenthal instead.

I have deliberately left out the soft cheeses such as Brie and Camembert, and the triple crèmes. This is not through any dislike of these magnificent products, but because they are scarcely ever used in conjunction with pasta. But don't let that hold you back if you should find yourself one day with some Boursin and some pasta. Go ahead and put the pasta into a pot of boiling water. Cut the creamy Boursin into small chunks. When the pasta is cooked and drained, toss it with the cheese and a good grinding of pepper. The cheese will melt into the pasta, and you will have a meal for the gods.

HARD CHEESE FOR GRATING

PARMIGIANO (PARMESAN)
The prototype: a hard, tangy cheese made from cow's milk in an area near Parma, Italy. The best grade is Reggiano but other Parmesans or grana, such as Padano, are (marginally) less expensive.

FONTINA
When matured this great Piedmontese cheese grates well.

31

CACIOCAVALLO
A white Italian curd cheese, made from cow's milk, which comes in a pear shape. Very similar to Provolone.

CHEDDAR
A mature farmhouse Cheddar can be used, grated, over pasta.

PECORINO
Pecorino is the family name for Italian sheep-milk cheeses, and there are a number available in Italian grocers: Romano, Sardo, Pugliese. It is much sharper than Parmesan.

PROVOLONE (MATURE)
The familiar sausage- and pear-shaped cheese wrapped in string, that hang from the ceiling in Italian groceries. Virtually the same as Caciocavallo and more common in Britain.

GOUDA (MATURE)
Made in Holland of cow's milk, it is usually soft, but it is sometimes available as a mature cheese which is hard and assertive in taste.

SBRINZ
Switzerland's Parmesan, occasionally available in good cheese shops.

MOIST, FRESH CHEESE

RICOTTA
A creamy, bland, rather sweet fresh Italian cheese. It may, *occasionally*, be found dried, when it can be grated.

COTTAGE CHEESE
A white, un-aged cheese made by draining off the whey that forms when cow's milk is heated.

CREAM CHEESE
A smooth, fresh cheese usually made from full cream milk, but should, of course, be made with cream, double or single.

CHÈVRE (GOAT CHEESE)

Fresh goat cheese becomes creamy when melted and adds a distinctive flavour to pasta.

BLUE CHEESE

GORGONZOLA

A soft, creamy cheese from Italy with a blue-green mould.

DOLCELATTE

A milder, creamier version of Gorgonzola, also from Italy.

DANISH BLUE OR DANABLU

A mild blue-mould cheese made in Denmark with cow's milk.

ROQUEFORT

The only blue-mould cheese made with sheep's milk, made in France, with a sharp and salty taste.

STILTON

The English 'King of cheeses', rich and creamy.

BLUE CHESHIRE

Another great English cheese, with a rich and unique flavour.

SEMI-SOFT AND NUTTY

EMMENTHAL

The model for all 'Swiss cheese': rubbery and mild, with round holes in the loaf.

GRUYÈRE

Smaller holes and a firmer, creamier texture than Emmenthal. From Switzerland.

APPENZELLER

Another cheese from Switzerland, it has no holes, and is quite rare in Britain.

JARLSBERG
An Emmenthal-type cheese from Norway, it is soft and smooth, with large holes in a creamy yellow body.

SAMSO
Danish cheese, related to Emmenthal.

FONTINA
A creamy, nutty, whole-fat cheese in a yellow waxy rind. From the mountains of Northern Italy near the Swiss border, it is sometimes still made with ewes' milk.

BUTTERY AND BLAND, FOR MELTING

MOZZARELLA
Originally made of buffalo milk, now of cow's milk. Shiny and sweet-tasting, and a dream to melt. Italian in its beginnings, it is now made all over the world, often specifically for pizzas.

LANCASHIRE
A crumbly and at times butter-like texture. This is one of the best English cheeses for cooking and melting.

MÜNSTER
Very creamy and very, very bland. Made in Germany, France, Switzerland and America.

EDAM
One of the two famous Dutch cheeses: semi-hard, in a cannonball shape with a red wax coating.

HAVARTI
A Danish cow's-milk cheese with a mild, sweet flavour.

TANGY AND CREAMY

CHESHIRE
An English cow's-milk cheese, deep orange or white in colour.

CHEDDAR
Originally from England, but now made throughout the world — excellent in quality, orange or white in colour.

CANTAL
A Cheddar-like cheese from France, made from cow's milk.

DOUBLE GLOUCESTER
'The golden cheese' once only made in Gloucestershire, where the cows give especially rich milk.

CAERPHILLY
A crumbly white cheese originally from Wales.

LEICESTER
A flaky-textured red-coloured cheese good for cooking.

WENSLEYDALE
A crumbly white to creamy yellow cheese (served with apple pie in the north of England).

WHAT TO DRINK WITH PASTA

You'll want to suit the wine to the sauce. If you're having fettuccine with butter and cheese, drink a glass of white wine with it. But if you're having a very heavy tomato sauce or a meat sauce, you'll probably prefer a red wine. A light Italian red wine is just the thing for seafood and tomato sauces, such as the linguine with tomato-shrimp sauce or the tuna variation on page 91.

With lo mein, pork with sauerkraut noodles (page 127), and curried beef sauce, nothing would be nicer than lots of cold beer. And with a first-course serving of pasta with caviar you might want a glass of champagne or, even better, vodka.

MAKING PASTA

BASIC PASTA RECIPE

This is the pasta I've been making for years. The recipe makes pale golden noodles with a wheaten taste and a nice resistance to the bite. It is simple enough to enjoy with only a nugget of unsalted butter and some grated cheese, but good enough to be the start of a complicated dish. Once you've learned the basic way, you'll vary the dough according to your imagination, maybe with spinach or maybe with tomato.

The ingredients are just flour, eggs and salt. If you mix the dough in the food processor or electric mixer, you will add a tablespoon of oil to the mixture just to get the machine going.

There are several ways to mix the dough and roll it out. By the old-fashioned method — and remember that pasta has been made since the beginning of civilisation — the dough is mixed on a wooden board, kneaded by hand, rolled and stretched paper-thin with a long wooden rolling pin, folded, cut and dried on a rack.

There are people who still swear that this method makes the best noodles. But now that there are so many mechanical aids available to us it would be foolish not to give them a try. I have had many splendid and quick meals of noodles that I made in the food processor and a pasta machine. I can start a tomato sauce cooking on the stove, toss flour, eggs and oil into the processor, and sit down, well within an hour, to a supper of freshly made linguine with a fiery shrimp and tomato sauce.

I'm going to tell you how to mix pasta dough by hand, in the electric mixer, and in the food processor. Then I'll describe rolling it out with a rolling pin and feeding it through the pasta machine. You will learn to cut noodles with a sharp knife, with a rolling pastry cutter, and with the cutting attachment of the machine. Finally, I will lead you through some of the new machines that promise to mix and extrude noodles all in one process.

My suggestion is that you try all the methods, and then choose the ones that work best for you. One person will enjoy getting his fingertips into the flour and egg, while another prefers the speed and manageability of the food processor. One finds hand rolling a great waste of effort, and another loves the feeling of mastery and control he gets from it. There's no way to know until you've tried them all. You may waste a dozen eggs along the way but, by the time you're done, you'll be a practised pasta maker.

If, however, you want to increase your chance of success the first time around, I suggest that you mix the dough in the electric mixer and roll it by machine. Dough that is blended in the mixer falls halfway between ultra-stiff hand-made dough and the slightly overheated mixture that comes out of the processor. And nothing will build your confidence like watching perfectly cut noodles falling out of the rollers of the pasta machine.

Another way to increase your chance of success is to learn the way pasta dough should feel. Having this recognition in your hands is as important as measuring properly. That's because you will be working with ingredients that change from day to day and from batch to batch. Some flours are drier than others; eggs vary in size; the air in your kitchen ranges from arid to muggy. A dough that works on a dry November day may refuse to roll out on a steamy August afternoon.

But, once your hands know how the dough should feel, it's easy to adapt the recipe to achieve that feeling. If it's too dry, you will sprinkle on some water or add a teaspoonful of beaten egg. If it's too damp, you can knead in extra flour. It's not unusual for me to add as much as 15 g (½ oz) of flour to the amount called for in the recipe.

The ideal, of course, would be to visit an experienced pasta maker and work under his supervision. Some Italians go so far as to say that no one can learn to make pasta who didn't start as a child in his mother's kitchen. But, since that chance is long gone for most of us, we'll have to rely on the trial-and-error method. It just requires some time and imagination.

To get an idea of what you're aiming for, think of the way that perfectly kneaded bread dough feels: plump, smooth and resilient under your palm. Then imagine a dough that's half again as stiff, and you'll have a pasta dough. It feels moist but not sticky when you poke a finger into it. And, when you knead it, it fights back more than bread dough does.

BASIC EGG PASTA

This makes enough pasta to serve 4 as an appetiser or 3 as a main course.

175 g (6 oz) flour
½ teaspoon salt
2 large eggs
1 tablespoon oil, if using the electric mixer
 or food processor

MIXING BY HAND

Put the flour mixed with the salt on a wooden board or another suitable work surface. Make a well in the centre of the mound, and break the eggs into the well. Beat the eggs with a fork, slowly incorporating the flour from the sides of the well. As you beat the eggs with one hand, your other hand should be shoring up the sides of the mound.

After a while, the paste will begin to clog the tines of the fork. Clean it off and continue to mix the flour into the egg mixture with your fingertips, just as you would in making any paste. When the flour and egg are all mixed, press the dough into a ball. It will seem to be composed of flakes of dough. Set it aside to rest for a minute while you wash your hands, scrape and clean the board, and dust it with flour. If there are dry flakes that obstinately refuse to become part of the mass, get rid of them now.

Now begin to knead the dough. Push the heel of your hand down hard, stretching the dough firmly away from you. Fold the flap back towards you and give the lump of dough a quarter-turn. Press down on another section of the dough.

Hand-mixed dough isn't easy to work with. It is stiff-textured and requires a lot of hard pummelling. At first it may seem that the ball of dough won't hold together, but the act of kneading will distribute the moisture evenly through it and, after a few minutes, it should begin to form a ball. Knead for a full ten minutes, pushing, folding, and turning until the dough is smooth. The thing to remember is that this is supposed to be harder than kneading bread, so don't despair. When you are done, pat the dough into a neat ball and cover it with a clean dish towel or a sheet of cling film. Let it rest for at least 30 minutes. Two hours' rest is even better.

MIXING BY ELECTRIC MIXER

Fit the paddle into your electric mixer. Put the flour and salt into the bowl, and give it a quick whirl to mix them. Add the eggs and oil and turn on the beater. Let it go for half a minute, until you have course grains of dough in the bowl, something like the consistency of pastry before it is gathered into a ball.

Replace the paddle with the dough hook and knead in the bowl for 5 minutes. Or take the dough from the bowl, dust a wooden surface with flour, pat the dough into a ball, and knead it for 10 minutes. You will find that this dough is much easier to work with than the hand-mixed dough. After 10 minutes, you should have a firm, smooth, pale yellow ball of dough. Put it to rest under a clean dish towel or in cling film.

41

MIXING BY FOOD PROCESSOR

Put the metal blade into the food processor. Measure in the flour and salt, and process briefly to blend them. Drop the eggs and oil through the feeding tube, and let the machine run until the dough begins to form a ball; around 15 seconds should do it. Once you've become familiar with the method, you'll be able to correct the recipe at this point. If the dough seems too sticky, add a tablespoon or two more flour. If it's too dry, add a few drops of water or part of an egg. Process again briefly.

Turn out the dough onto a floured surface. You will notice that this method results in the yellowest and stickiest dough of all. That's because it's already half-kneaded. Dust your hands with flour and continue the kneading. Work for 3 to 5 minutes, adding more flour if necessary, until you have a smooth ball of dough. Set it to rest under a clean dish towel or in cling film.

RESTING I

I cannot emphasise too strongly the importance of letting the dough rest between the kneading and the rolling. During this period, which should last at least 30 minutes and can continue in the refrigerator for days, the gluten in the flour relaxes and the dough becomes soft, well blended, and easy to work. I've put many a worrisome dough to rest under a clean dish towel, only to retrieve it 2 hours later, in perfect condition for rolling.

ROLLING BY HAND

There are two stages in rolling pasta by hand. In the first, the dough is worked just as it is when you are making pastry, pressing down and out from the centre. This usually presents no problem for most cooks.

The second stage is harder to learn, because you have to be able to do two things at once. It's a little like learning to pat your head and rub your stomach at the same time: once you get it, it's easy; but the first few times you try to do it, it seems impossible.

To begin, place the ball of dough on a floured surface. Pat it into a flat circle and start to roll it with your rolling pin. Move always from the centre to the edges of the circle, giving the dough a quarter-turn after each roll to keep the circular shape. Keep checking to be sure that the dough isn't sticking to the board. If it is, loosen with a dough scraper and dust with flour. When the dough is about 6 mm (¼ inch) thick, the first stage is finished.

During the second stage, you will be pulling and stretching the dough instead of rolling it. Very often, I've seen experienced pasta rollers hang one end of the sheet over the edge of the table and lean their tummies against it as they roll. That way, they get a three-way action, pulling, rolling and stretching!

Curl the far edge of the circle around the centre of your rolling pin. Then roll the pin back toward you, wrapping some of the dough around it. Push and stretch it away from you as you unroll the dough. At the same time, slide your hands lightly out and in on the pin, stretching the sheet sideways. Don't press down. Pull out.

Turn the circle slightly after each stretch. You are trying to make a very thin sheet of dough, something like the thickness of good writing paper. It will be slightly transparent. You won't be able to read through it, but if you're rolling on a wooden surface, you should be able to see the grain of wood through the dough.

One way to be sure that you're rolling the dough evenly and that it isn't sticking to the board is to check its colour. If the colour is more intense at the centre of the circle than at the edges, it means that the dough is thicker there. That often happens when it has stuck to the board. Roll it up onto the pin (a dough scraper will be helpful). Dust the board with flour. Turn the dough face down and flour its top side. Rub some flour onto the rolling pin.

If the business of stretching and pulling and sliding your hands in and out seems too much for you to master, you can roll out the dough as you might a very thin pastry. It takes a lot of work, because you'll be fighting the gluten's elasticity, but it can definitely be done.

ROLLING BY MACHINE

There are two kinds of wringer-style pasta machines — one that is turned by hand, and one that is operated by a motor. Each has its advantages and its fans.

The hand-cranked model is considerably cheaper than the motorised machine. And it is my opinion that many people are intimidated by the speed with which the motor-driven machine processes the dough. They like the feeling of being in control that they get from turning the handle themselves.

Other people prefer the speed and efficiency of the motorised machine. They feel that there are never enough hands around to do everything that has to be done with a hand-cranked machine.

All of the machines work on the same principle. The dough is fed through a set of cylindrical rollers, which knead it, flatten it and, when the rollers have been changed, cut it into strips.

After the ball of dough has rested for a few hours, cut it into four pieces. Put three of them back under the cloth, and flatten the fourth with a rolling pin or with your palm. Set the machine so that the rollers are at their widest opening.

If you are using the electric model, turn on the machine (it will make an infernal racket); otherwise start cranking. Feed the flattened ball of dough through the rollers four or five times, folding it in half each time before it goes back through the rollers. This will further knead and smooth the dough.

It may come out with ragged edges or with holes torn in it. This often happens when the dough hasn't been kneaded enough. Don't worry. Patch the holes with bits torn from the end, and feed the dough back through the rollers. If the edges are ragged, fold the ribbon in half lengthwise. If the dough comes out in a distorted shape, just fold it up into a flat square and roll it through again. You'll know when it's rolled enough, because the dough will become smooth and satiny. The nice thing about pasta dough is that it isn't one of those delicate mixtures that shouldn't be overhandled. Go ahead and work with it. It thrives on the human touch.

Now begin to narrow the opening between the rollers by turning the dial one mark each time the dough goes through. Keep going until you reach the thickness you want. Then make a note of the number on the dial, and you'll have something to aim for the next time you roll out pasta.

Lay the ribbon of pasta on a clean dish towel while you roll out the other three pieces of dough.

RESTING II

Once the dough has been rolled out, it should lie on kitchen towels for around 5 minutes to give it a chance to dry. Machine-rolled dough dries faster than hand-rolled, so the first ribbons will probably be ready to cut by the time the last ones are rolled. Don't let it get too dry, however. The dough should be pliable, neither brittle nor moist and sticky. If it just doesn't dry, dust it with some more flour and no harm will be done.

CUTTING BY HAND

There are two ways to cut simple noodles by hand. The easier is to fold the dough and cut it into slices with a sharp knife. It's very important that the dough should be well dried if you use this method, or it will stick to itself when it is folded.

Take one edge of the dough and fold it over loosely into a flat roll about 7.5 cm (3 inches) wide. Continue to fold until the whole strip or circle of dough is folded. Then take a sharp knife or cleaver and cut 6—12-mm (¼—½-inch) slices from the rolled dough. Don't saw. Press down evenly, trying to make the slices even in width. As soon as the whole roll has been cut, open up the noodles so they can dry further.

You can also cut noodles with a rolling pastry cutter. I have one that George Lang gave me that cuts four noodles at a time. Most pastry wheels are single, however, and the problem with using them is that you have to have a very steady hand and a good eye to make the noodles come out even in width.

CUTTING BY MACHINE

You can use the pasta machine to cut both the hand-rolled and the machine-rolled dough. If you have a circle of hand-rolled dough, just cut the circle into 10—11-cm (4½-inch) strips that will fit through the machine.

If you are using the electric model, remove the smooth rollers from the machine and fit one of the cutting attachments into place. For the hand-cranked model, insert the handle into one of the cutting slots. Turn on the motor or begin to turn the handle, and feed the ribbons of dough into the right side of the machine. They will come out on the left side in nicely cut strands. If the machine doesn't cut them all the way through, your dough is probably too sticky, and you should set it aside to dry out a little longer.

DRYING

At this point you can simply drop the freshly cut pasta into boiling water. But it is probably more convenient to get the work of making pasta out of the way a little while before mealtime. And many Italians, I ought to mention, feel that drying is an essential step in the making of pasta; that omitting it changes the quality of the pasta. I can't say that I agree, but it is certainly more convenient to make your pasta early in the day and dry it out.

Take up strands of pasta and loop them loosely around your fingers, forming nests. Let them dry on a cloth or on a cake rack.

You can really use anything to dry pasta on — a broomstick, the back of a chair, a clothes-line. I've been in Italian kitchens where the fettucine hung like a curtain from a clothes-line — strung across the corner of the kitchen. You might want to use one of those two- or three-tiered clothes driers that were designed to stand in the bath. I happen to have a marvellous pasta rack that was made for me by a friend. Unfortunately, it isn't available commercially. It's an upright pole with a disc on the top. Three wooden rods fit into holes on the disc. I drape the pasta over the rods. Then, when I want to cook it, I simply pull off one of the rods, carry it to the stove, and push the pasta into the boiling water.

Once the pasta is really dry, you can put it in a tin and store it just as though it were commercial spaghetti. Be careful when you handle it: it will be very brittle. Or you can put the rolled-up nests into plastic bags and stick them in the freezer. But, once you've gone to all the trouble of making it, you will probably just want to cook it.

COOKING

The point to remember about home-made pasta is that it cooks in no time at all. Dried home-made pasta takes a little longer than the truly freshly made, but even so it will be done practically as soon as the water returns to the boil. *Have your sauce ready* before you put the pasta anywhere near the water. And don't pay attention to any recipe that tells you to cook pasta for 8 to 10 minutes. This is too long, even for most commercial brands.

(Although I have to say that cooking is the one inexplicable art in pasta making. I find that there is absolutely no way to figure it out when you use commercial pastas. You put it in the pot, and you taste it after 4 minutes, and then after 8 minutes, and finally in desperation after 12 minutes, and it still has the crunch in the middle.)

Have lots of water boiling furiously. I don't add any salt, because I think that your sauce and cheese will provide enough seasoning. But it's a good idea to add a splash of oil to keep the strands from sticking together.

Drop the home-made pasta into the boiling water. Start testing it as soon as it returns to the boil. I've heard all kinds of methods for testing pasta, but the best one is just to fish out a strand and bite into it. If the noodle is beautifully pliable, with no hard core to it, then your pasta is done. Pour the contents of the pot into a colander in the sink, and get ready to mix in your sauce.

VARIATIONS
The same recipe can be used to make different-coloured pastas and to incorporate different grains and flavours.

● **Green Pasta:** Add 225-g (½-lb) fresh spinach, wilted and squeezed dry, or half of a 300-g (10-oz) packet frozen spinach, defrosted and squeezed dry, to the flour, salt and olive oil. Use only 1 egg.

● **Tomato Pasta:** Add 2 tablespoons tomato purée to the flour, salt and olive oil. Use 1½ eggs. Add one to the flour, beat the second in a measuring cup, and pour half of it into the flour mixture.

● **Beetroot Pasta:** This makes a beautiful scarlet dough. The amount of grated beetroot you add depends on the richness of colour you desire. Start by adding 2 tablespoons grated cooked or bottled beetroot to the basic recipe.

● **Golden Pasta:** This comes from my friend Jim Nassikas, the director of the Stanford Court Hotel in San Francisco. Using the basic recipe, add 7 egg yolks instead of the 2 eggs. If you have trouble making the dough hold together, add an eighth egg yolk.

● **Basil Pasta:** To the basic recipe add 3 tablespoons of a simple Pesto (see page 70).

48

- **Whole-wheat Pasta:** I like this whole-wheat pasta. It's very rich tasting. Instead of 175-g (6-oz) flour, use 150-g (5-oz) whole-wheat flour and 25-g (1-oz) plain flour. Have on hand another 25-g (1-oz) plain flour to knead in as necessary.
- **Buckwheat Pasta:** Instead of 175-g (6-oz) flour, use 75-g (3-oz) buckwheat flour and 50-g (2-oz) plain flour. Have on hand another 25-g (1-oz) plain flour to knead in as necessary. (Buckwheat flour is available in health-food shops.)
- **Carl Sontheimer's Parmesan Pasta:** To the basic recipe add 75-g (3-oz) grated Parmesan cheese.

FRENCH NOODLES

Nine egg yolks make this dough so rich that in order to knead it you first have to do a *fraisage*, a special method of blending butter-rich pâte brisée. Once this is done, the noodles are kneaded like any other pasta dough. It makes noodles that are very delicate, although extremely rich in ingredients. I think this is one of the best pastas I have ever tasted.

6 TO 8 SERVINGS
450-g (1-lb) flour, preferably strong white
or semolina
1 teaspoon salt
3 eggs
6 egg yolks
2 tablespoons water

Mix the dough as you did in the basic recipe. Make a mound of flour and salt, open a hollow in its centre, break in the eggs, yolks and water, and then combine with a fork until you are forced to continue mixing by hand.

When you have formed the dough into a rough ball and cleaned off the table you begin the *fraisage*. Pull off walnut-

49

sized pieces of dough, and push them away from you under the heel of your hand, smearing them on the board one at a time. When all the dough has been worked this way, gather the bits back into a ball, using the pastry scraper to help. The *fraisage* will have blended the fat and flour so that the dough can be kneaded. Knead well, and let rest 1 to 2 hours before you roll it out.

This dough keeps very well so if you don't want to use all of it right away, just refrigerate it, wrapped in cling film, and tear off a piece as wanted; it will keep for several days.

EGG-WHITE NOODLES

Pasta is actually a low-fat main course, especially when it is served with a simple tomato sauce. But, for those people who can't even take the cholesterol that is contributed by the egg yolks in the noodles, here is a noodle made with no yolks — ergo, no cholesterol — and with one tiny tablespoonful of olive oil.

6 TO 8 SERVINGS
450-g (1-lb) flour
1 teaspoon salt
1 tablespoon olive oil
7 to 8 egg whites

Put the metal chopping blade in place in the bowl of the food processor. Add the flour, salt and oil, and process for 8 to 10 seconds. Add the egg whites and process about 15 seconds, until the dough is pliable but not damp or sticky. Knead by hand for a few minutes, then let rest and roll out by hand or in the pasta machine.

50

BARBARA KAFKA'S BUCKWHEAT NOODLES

This recipe was given me by Barbara Kafka, an imaginative and creative cook. It's different from my own method (see page 49) of making buckwheat noodles because it has no eggs, and because the presence of lager and yeast makes the noodles very light.

Buckwheat flour is to be found in good health-food shops.

> 3 TO 4 SERVINGS
> *100-ml (4-fl oz) lager, at room temperature*
> *1 teaspoon dried yeast*
> *25-g (1-oz) buckwheat flour*
> *100-g (4-oz) plain flour*
> *¼ teaspoon sea salt*

In a small bowl, combine half the lager, the yeast, and 2 tablespoons of the buckwheat flour. Stir to make a sponge, cover and let rise in a warm place for at least an hour.

Stir in the rest of the buckwheat flour, the white flour, salt and 2 tablespoons of the remaining lager. Use only enough lager to make a soft but firm dough. You will probably not use the whole amount. Cover again, and let the dough rest for 30 minutes.

Divide it into quarters and roll it out by hand or in the pasta machine. Don't hesitate to flour the dough if it seems sticky as you work it. Cut into medium-width noodles.

UDON NOODLES

I am indebted to Elizabeth Andoh's Japanese mother-in-law for this recipe. Because the dough is made without eggs or oil, it is very stiff, and the best way to knead it is to wrap it in a few layers of plastic bags and then tread on it. It's great fun to make, and produces thick snow-white noodles that are traditionally used in soup. Udon flour is a combination

51

of unbleached flours available occasionally in Japanese and other oriental grocers. They all, however, sell the noodles themselves, sometimes accompanied by the soup base.

4 SERVINGS
1 tablespoon salt
150-ml (5-fl oz) water
350-g (12-oz) udon flour

Add the salt to the water and stir until it is dissolved. Put the flour in a bowl and pour in the salt water. Stir lightly until the mixture is crumbly. Form it into a ball (this will not be easy). Put it in a plastic bag to rest for 30 minutes, or refrigerate for several hours.

Now the fun begins. Put the plastic-wrapped dough into a very sturdy plastic bag. In Mrs Andoh's book, *At Home with Japanese Cooking*, she recommends stamping on the dough with the whole of your foot. We found that the best method was to tiptoe with the ball of the foot in what seemed a very Japanese manner. When the dough becomes flat, open up the bags and fold it into a ball again. Repeat until the dough is smooth and satiny: at least 5 minutes. Finally, stamp the dough into an oval about 6 mm (¼ inch) in thickness.

(If the whole process seems silly to you, you can knead the dough by hand for 10 to 15 minutes if you have the strength, or process it with a dough hook. But I do hope you'll try the stepping technique.)

Roll out the dough on a floured board, stretching it into a large oval. Make 4 or 5 pleated folds, and cut the dough into 6-mm (¼-inch) wide ribbons with a cleaver or a sharp knife.

BREAD NOODLES

These are fun, an unusual noodle made of yeast-rising bread dough. It's a good, solid accompaniment to any meat with a sauce, nice with Irish stew, even better with the Instant Beef Bourguignon you'll find on page 370 of *The New James Beard*. The recipe makes enough dough so that half of it can be used for noodles and the other half for crunchy bread sticks.

4 SERVINGS
300-g (10-oz) flour
½ teaspoon salt
¾ teaspoon dry yeast
225-ml (8-fl oz) warm water
1 egg white beaten with 1 tablespoon water
  and ½ teaspoon salt
Sesame seeds

In a mixing bowl, blend the flour, salt, yeast, and warm water. Turn out the dough onto a lightly floured board and knead it for 15 minutes. You may have to add extra flour to make a stiff but supple dough. Put it into an oiled mixing bowl, turning so that it is coated with the oil. Cover with cling film and allow to rise in a warm place until it has doubled in bulk, about 1 hour.

Punch down the dough. Return half to the bowl and take the other half to make into bread sticks. With a knife, cut the dough into 8 equal pieces. Using your palms, roll each piece into a thin cylinder about 20-cm (8-inches) long. Cut each one in half and place them, 2.5-cm (1-inch) apart, on an oiled baking sheet. Let them sit for 20 minutes, until they just begin to soften in contour. Brush with the egg glaze, sprinkle with sesame seeds, and bake for 20 to 25 minutes at 150°C (300°F) Gas 2. The longer they cook, the crisper they will become.

Meanwhile, punch down the rest of the dough again. Run it through the pasta machine several times, dusting it with flour if it feels sticky. Begin to narrow the opening of the machine and continue until the dough is quite thin. Change the rollers and cut the dough into noodles. Lay them on a wooden board or dish towel to rise slightly while you bring a pot of water to the boil. Drop the noodles into the boiling water. Test for doneness as soon as the water returns to the boil. Drain in a colander and serve with a hearty meat-based sauce and a basket of sesame-studded bread sticks.

BULGARIAN SHREDDED NOODLES

This unusual recipe may well be the oldest form of pasta we have. It comes from Bulgaria, but there are noodles like it in modern Hungarian cooking, where they are called *trahana*. I think that these balls of dough were once carried in the saddlebags of nomadic horsemen, then grated into pots of water when they made camp for the night. I make them with a strong, salty Caciocavallo cheese that's similar to the Bulgarian cheese called Kashkaval.

4 TO 6 SERVINGS
2 eggs
1 teaspoon salt
200-g (7-oz) flour
225-ml (8-fl oz) water
225-ml (8-fl oz) milk
25-g (1-oz) butter
50—75-g (2—3-oz) grated cheese

Beat the eggs and ½ teaspoon of the salt in a bowl. Add the flour, mixing with a wooden spoon until it is incorporated. Begin to knead in the bowl, and, when all the flour has been mixed in, turn the dough out onto a flat surface. Knead for 3 to 4 minutes more, until the dough is firm, stiff, and very smooth. Form it into a ball, wrap it in cling film, and freeze. This should take at least half a day, but it can, of course, then remain in the freezer for weeks.

When the ball of dough is frozen hard, cover a large area of your working surface or table with sheets of grease-

54

proof paper. Holding a grater over the paper, shred the dough through its largest holes, moving the grater back and forth so that the shreds don't fall on top of each other. When you're done, scatter and separate the bits of pasta so that they won't stick together. Let the shreds dry out on the paper. Once they're completely dry, you can gather them onto a single sheet of paper and store as you would any pasta.

To cook the shreds: Heat the water, milk, remaining salt, and half the butter in a saucepan. Bring to a boil and sprinkle in the pasta slowly so that the liquid remains at the boil. Lower the heat and simmer for a few minutes, uncovered, until the pasta is firmly cooked and all the liquid is absorbed. Turn it into a baking dish and dot with the remaining butter. Dry out in a 110°C (225°F), Gas ¼ oven for 10 to 14 minutes. Just before serving, toss it with lots of grated cheese.

SPÄTZLE

Spätzle are tiny dumplings, bits of dough that are never rolled out but are simply dropped into boiling water, and keep whatever shape they happen into when the water hits them. I've tried two kinds of spätzle makers. One looks rather like a food mill: a circular metal bowl with a flat perforated base and a blade that goes around and around over the base. The other is a rectangular sieve, something like a grater, with a bowl that slides back and forth over it. In both cases, the dough is spooned into the bowl and falls through the large holes on the bottom, being cut off either by the turn of the blade or by the movement over the grater.

But the fact is that you don't need either of these contraptions to make spätzle. I suspect that the original spätzle makers just dropped bits of dough off the tip of a spoon into boiling water or chopped bits off a damp board with a wet knife.

The most elegant spätzle I've ever had was at the Four Seasons Restaurant in New York, where it came with a rabbit paprikash. Use them with beef stew or veal goulash. Or go mad and have them with chili. They'd be wonderful, just the right combination of blandness, starchiness, and chew.

4 SERVINGS
65—75-g (2½—3-oz) strong white bread flour
  or semolina
1 egg
50-ml (2-fl oz) warm water or milk

Measure the flour into a bowl. Add the egg and beat it with a wooden spoon, incorporating the flour. Add the liquid and continue to stir briskly until you have a stiff batter. Put it aside to rest for 15 minutes. It will become even stiffer.

Get your cooking liquid to a rapid boil. If you have a spätzle maker, place it over the boiling liquid, spoon in the batter, and turn the crank or slide the carriage back and forth. Pear-shaped drops of batter will fall into the liquid, rising to the surface as they cook. Skim them off with a slotted spoon, and put them in a warm bowl with a lump of unsalted butter. If you don't have a spätzle maker, pick up bits of batter on the tip of a teaspoon and flick them off into the boiling water with a second spoon.

SPATZEN

I'm not sure why this dish is called *spatzen* and the other is called *spätzle*. I suspect that it depends on what side of the street or what district of Vienna you lived in. The ingredients are slightly different, but the technique remains the same.

4 SERVINGS
75-g (3-oz) flour
Pinch baking powder
Pinch salt
1 egg
60-ml (2½-fl oz) water, approximately

Combine the flour, baking powder, and salt in a bowl. Stir in the egg with a wooden spoon, and add enough of the water to make a stiff batter. Set it aside to rest for 15 minutes. Then cook the spatzen by dropping bits of batter into boiling liquid through a spätzle maker or from the tip of a spoon. Drain, mix with unsalted butter, and serve either with gravy or with grated cheese.

NOCKERLI

Nockerli are tiny dumplings made by pinching off bits of dough and rolling them into tiny balls. They are nice cooked in a rich beef broth, or mixed with a hearty vegetable, as in the pasta with cabbage on page 82.

8 SERVINGS
2 eggs
350-g (12-oz) flour
1 teaspoon salt
15-g (½-oz) butter, melted
175-ml (6-fl oz) water

In a large bowl, mix the eggs, flour, and salt. Add the melted butter and water and beat with a wooden spoon for 4 minutes. Let sit for at least 20 minutes. Then, using your lightly floured hands, pinch off bits of dough, roll them gently between your palms, and drop them into boiling water or broth. They are done when they float to the top.

POTATO GNOCCHI

I love gnocchi. To me, they're sort of magic. They have that soul-satisfying potato-ey, floury quality, and with a sauce they are just wonderful.

6 TO 8 SERVINGS
900-g (2-lb) potatoes
225-g (8-oz) flour
2 eggs
25-g (1-oz) butter
½ teaspoon salt
¾ teaspoon freshly ground black pepper
65-g (2½-oz) butter, melted
Grated Parmesan or Caciocavallo cheese

Peel and quarter the potatoes. Boil them in salted water until they can be pierced with a fork. Drain, return to the pan, and mash. Set the pan over a very low flame, and dry out the potatoes, stirring occasionally, until they are no longer gummy. This may take as long as 10 minutes. You can also bake the potatoes in a 230°C (450°F), Gas 8 oven until they are done, then cut them in half lengthwise and put them back into the turned-off oven to dry for 10 minutes. Remove the insides and mash them with a fork. (If you use this method, I need hardly mention, you get to eat all the crisp potato skins!)

Put the mashed potatoes in a mixing bowl and beat in the flour, eggs, butter, salt, and pepper. When all the ingredients are incorporated, turn the dough out onto a work surface and knead it gently for 3 minutes. It will be very soft. Spill a pile of flour onto the work surface, and use it to coat your hands while you work with the gnocchi. Pull off a lump of dough the size of a lemon and roll it into a long sausage as wide as your finger. Work from the centre out, trying to make the roll even in width. Continue until you have rolled all the dough. Then, using a knife or your dough scraper, cut the dough into pieces about 2-cm (¾-inch) long. With the back of a knife or fork, make a slight diagonal indentation and fold it in toward the dent. Roll the gnocchi gently under the tines of a fork so that they are ridged.

Bring a large pot of water to the boil. Drop the gnocchi into the water about 8 at a time, and cook them for 3 to 4 minutes, until they float to the top. Remove with a slotted spoon, and arrange in a buttered baking dish. Pour on the melted butter and sprinkle with grated cheese. Heat in a 180°C (350°F), Gas 4 oven for 15 to 20 minutes. If you make the gnocchi early in the day, you can get them ready in the pan and then reheat them for 30 minutes in the oven.

VARIATIONS
- To the basic dough add about 20-g (¾-oz) chopped fresh basil and 20-g (¾-oz) chopped fresh chives.
- To the basic dough add 50-g (2-oz) grated Gruyère cheese and a large pinch of mace.
- Spread about two-thirds of the recipe for Light Tomato Sauce (page 71) over the cooked gnocchi arranged in the baking dish and sprinkle liberally with Parmesan cheese, then bake as above.

GNOCCHI VERDI

These are sometimes called *malfatti*, which means 'badly made', because they are so delicate that when they are cooked they are quite uneven in shape. You have to skim them out of the water very, very carefully because of their fragility, but they well repay the care: they just melt on your tongue when you eat them.

59

6 SERVINGS

350-g (12-oz) cooked spinach, drained and
*   chopped (approximately 450—550-g or*
*   1—1¼-lb fresh spinach, or two 300-g or*
*   10-oz packets frozen spinach)*
½ teaspoon salt
Freshly ground black pepper
⅛ teaspoon nutmeg
15-g (½-oz) butter
225-g (8-oz) Ricotta cheese
2 eggs
40-g (1½-oz) Parmesan cheese, grated
3 tablespoons flour

SAUCE:
100-g (4-oz) butter, melted
40-g (1½-oz) grated Parmesan cheese

Put the spinach in a saucepan with the salt, pepper, nutmeg, butter, and Ricotta. Stir it over low heat for about 5 minutes to dry it out. Remove from the heat and beat in the eggs, Parmesan, and the flour. Set the mixture aside to cool for 2 hours.

Dust a wooden board and your hands with flour. Pull off walnut-sized pieces of the spinach mixture, and form croquettes the shape of a cork. Roll them in the flour and, when they are all ready, drop them carefully into a large pot of very gently simmering water. Don't let the water boil, or the action may cause the gnocchi to disintegrate. If the mixture seems too soft, don't worry, because the eggs and flour will hold the gnocchi together when they come in contact with the simmering water.

When the gnocchi rise to the surface of the water, they have finished cooking. Skim them off with a slotted spoon, drain them well, and place them in an ovenproof baking dish lightly coated with butter. Pour the melted butter over them, sprinkle with the Parmesan cheese, and heat in a 180°C (350°F), Gas 4 oven for 20 to 30 minutes.

PASTAS IN SOUP

CHINESE NOODLE SOUP
UDON NOODLE SOUP
PORTUGUESE FISH STEW

CHINESE NOODLE SOUP

My first memory of eating noodles was in a dish much like this one. It also had, as I remember, strips of ham and spring onion and delicate bits of egg pancake floating on top, so feel free to add anything you like to the broth. Since that time, by the way, I've always considered noodles one of the standard soup vegetables. Best of all, for this soup, are the fresh Chinese noodles that are sold in Chinese supermarkets and grocers.

4 TO 6 SERVINGS
about 1.4 litres (2½-pt) good home-made
  chicken stock
1 tablespoon soy sauce
¼ teaspoon Tabasco
100-g (4-oz) Chinese noodles

Bring the chicken stock to a simmer. Season it with soy sauce and Tabasco. Rinse the noodles and lower them into the pot so that the boiling never stops. When the noodles are cooked, ladle some stock and noodles into each bowl.

VARIATION
● For the egg pancake, mix yolk and white together briefly. Cook in frying pan, turning once to set. Roll each up like a crêpe and cut in thin strips to garnish noodles and broth. 1 egg per serving.

UDON NOODLE SOUP

A Japanese speciality is hearty soups full of thick, slippery udon noodles. Make them yourself, following the recipe on page 51, or buy them in a Japanese or Oriental grocers. And be sure that the broth is dense with good things to eat.

4 TO 6 SERVINGS
about 1.4 litres (2½-pt) cold water
675-g (1½-lb) chicken pieces
6 slices fresh ginger root
*2 leeks, washed, including 5-cm (2-inches) of
   the green*
1½ teaspoons salt
½ teaspoon freshly ground black pepper
2 egg whites, beaten
100-g (4-oz) udon noodles
1 bunch radishes, thinly sliced
*1 bunch spring onions, thinly sliced on the
   diagonal, including 5-cm (2-inches) of
   the green*
100-g (4-oz) Chinese leaves, thinly sliced

Put the water in a very large pot with the chicken pieces. Add the ginger, leeks, salt, and freshly ground black pepper. Bring the water to a boil over high heat, skim off the froth that rises to the top, and simmer 30 to 45 minutes, partially covered.

Line a colander with several layers of cheesecloth and pour the hot broth through it into a bowl. Discard the chicken bones, skin, meat and vegetables, wash out your stock-pot, and return the soup to the pot. Bring to a boil and swirl in the beaten egg whites. When the broth returns to the boil, remove from the heat, and strain it again through a colander lined with cheesecloth.

Cook the noodles in boiling water until they are done. Rinse well, and place them, with the radishes, spring onions, and Chinese leaves, in individual soup bowls. Ladle the hot stock over the vegetables and serve at once.

PORTUGUESE FISH STEW

This is one of my favourite soups, a hearty main-course dish that could be served to friends with bread, cheese, and fruit. It is related to the San Francisco speciality cioppino. I especially like it with orzo, a tiny granular pasta that looks just like rice, but any tiny pasta would do.

4 TO 6 SERVINGS
800-g (28-oz) tin Italian plum tomatoes
2 small onions, sliced
5 cloves garlic, chopped
6 leaves fresh basil, or 1 teaspoon dried basil
Salt and freshly ground black pepper
4 tablespoons olive oil
850-ml (1½-pt) chicken stock
450-g (1-lb) peeled cooked shrimps
  or prawns
450-g (1-lb) fresh tuna, cut in 1-cm
  (½-inch) strips
175-g (6-oz) orzo

In a very large pot, cook the tomatoes, onions, garlic, basil, salt, and pepper over medium heat for 20 minutes, stirring frequently. Add the oil. Strain or process the sauce and return it to the pot. Add the chicken stock, bring to a boil, and let it simmer for 10 minutes. The soup can be done ahead of time to this point.

When you are ready to serve the soup, bring it back to the boil. Put in the shrimps and the strips of raw tuna, and turn off the heat immediately.

Cook the orzo in boiling water. In the bottoms of 4 to 6 soup bowls, put a large spoonful of cooked orzo. Ladle over the orzo portions of soup containing some shrimps and some fish.

MAINLY VEGETABLE

VEGETABLE SAUCES

PESTO
(freezer · with walnuts · with parsley)

LIGHT TOMATO SAUCE
(with other herbs)

FRESH TOMATO SAUCE

MUSHROOM-TOMATO SAUCE

SPINACH-ANCHOVY SAUCE

BRAISED ONION SAUCE

MUSHROOM SAUCE

HERBED BUTTER SAUCE

PASTA PRIMAVERA

SAUTÉED VEGETABLES WITH SPÄTZLE

SPAGHETTINI WITH ASPARAGUS

FETTUCCINE WITH COURGETTES

SPAGHETTINI WITH FRIED AUBERGINE

PASTA ESTIVI

TURNIP GREENS WITH PINE KERNELS

PASTA WITH PARSLEY PESTO

NOODLES WITH CABBAGE

VEGETABLE-NOODLE CASSEROLE

PASTA WITH BEANS

AVOCADO PASTA

VEGETABLE SAUCES

I'm beginning the section of vegetable dishes with 8 sauces, all based on herbs or vegetables, to be served over pasta. Most of them are just right for 350-g (12-oz) of pasta, that is, for 3 or 4 main-course servings. The pesto recipe makes a great deal more than that, but then in the summer, when fresh basil is available, you should get as much as you can for making pesto and freezing for the winter ahead. The Light Tomato Sauce is another one of those resource sauces that are perfectly good served plain, but that can also be turned into a nearly infinite number of variations.

PESTO

I have basil plants growing in pots in the garden behind my house. I chop the fresh leaves onto summer tomatoes, and every so often I harvest a lot of leaves and make pesto. With pesto in the freezer, I can recover the fragrance of summer in my kitchen all winter long. Use it on plain pasta — you'll need about 175-g (6-oz) for 225-g (8-oz) — or to flavour soups, stews, and salad dressings.

> MAKES ABOUT 350-g (12-oz)
> *225-g (8-oz) basil leaves*
> *3 cloves garlic*
> *150-g (5-oz) pine kernels*
> *25-g (1-oz) flat-leaved (or Continental) parsley*
> *1 teaspoon salt*
> *125—225-ml (4—8-fl oz) olive oil*
> *40—50-g (1½—2-oz) Pecorino or Parmesan*
>   *cheese, coarsely grated*

Put the basil, garlic, pine kernels, parsley, and salt into the food processor or blender with 125-ml (4-fl oz) oil. Process,

70

adding enough additional oil to make a smooth paste. Add the cheese and process a few seconds longer.

VARIATIONS

- **Freezer Pesto:** To make pesto for the freezer, just process the basil, garlic, parsley, salt, and oil. Freeze it in 175-g (6-oz) portions. When you are ready to use it, defrost the sauce and put it back into the processor with the pine kernels and cheese. If you want to use it as a seasoning, you can eliminate the kernels and cheese and simply chip off teaspoonfuls of puréed pesto from the frozen mass.
- **Pesto with Walnuts:** Instead of the pine kernels, use 50-g (2-oz) walnuts and omit the cheese.
- **Pesto with Parsley:** Instead of basil, use 175-g (6-oz) flat-leaved parsley for a fresh midwinter pesto.

✓ LIGHT TOMATO SAUCE

I am reprinting this recipe, which was in *The New James Beard*, because it forms the basis for a nearly limitless number of variations. It also has the advantage of using tinned tomatoes, so that you aren't dependent on the season or the quality of the tomatoes in your market.

> MAKES ABOUT 675-g (1½-lb)
> *800-g (28-oz) tin Italian plum tomatoes*
> *2 small onions, sliced*
> *Salt and freshly ground black pepper to taste*
> *1 teaspoon dried basil (optional)*
> *50-g (2-oz) butter*

Cook the tomatoes, onions, salt, pepper, and basil over medium-high heat for 20 minutes, stirring frequently. If you want a smooth sauce, strain it or purée it in the food processor. I prefer to leave the sauce with lumps, just breaking up the tomatoes with a wooden spoon. Then add the butter and continue to cook until it melts.

71

VARIATION
- Instead of the basil, substitute 1 teaspoon dried oregano or tarragon or any other herb that you fancy.

FRESH TOMATO SAUCE

ENOUGH FOR 675-g (1½-lb) PASTA
50-g (2-oz) unsalted butter
1 medium onion, sliced
1.1-kg (2½-lb) tomatoes, peeled, seeded,
 and chopped
2 teaspoons salt
1 tablespoon chopped fresh basil, or
 1 teaspoon dried basil, or ½ teaspoon
 mixed dried herbs (optional)
Grated cheese

Melt the butter in a heavy saucepan. Add the onion and sauté over medium heat until soft and transparent. Add the tomatoes, salt, and herbs and simmer gently for 10 minutes. Pour over freshly cooked pasta, mix well, and sprinkle with grated cheese.

MUSHROOM–TOMATO SAUCE

MAKES ABOUT 675-g (1½-lb)
1 recipe Light Tomato Sauce (p. 71),
 without the butter
225-g (8-oz) mushrooms, thinly sliced
50-g (2-oz) unsalted butter

Cook the tomato sauce. While it simmers, sauté the mushrooms in butter, and add them to the sauce for the final 5 minutes of cooking.

SPINACH–ANCHOVY SAUCE

Try this on spaghettini or angel's hair to wake up the appetite at the beginning of a meal.

MAKES ABOUT 900-g (2-lb)
1 recipe Light Tomato Sauce (p. 71),
  without the butter
25-g (1-oz) butter
2 cloves garlic, finely chopped
225-g (8-oz) chopped cooked spinach
4 anchovies, cut in small pieces
3 tablespoons pine kernels, toasted

Cook the tomato sauce. While it simmers, melt the butter and cook the garlic until it is golden brown. Stir in the spinach and anchovies, stir over medium heat for a few minutes, and then add to the tomato sauce.

Toss well, then add the toasted nuts, and serve.

 # BRAISED ONION SAUCE

Long-cooked onions have a naturally sweet taste. This is a substantial sauce, and I like to serve it with a pasta that has body, something like pasta bows or wheels, or wide ribbons or macaroni.

ENOUGH FOR 350–450-g (12–16-oz) PASTA
225-g (½-lb) unsalted butter
675-g (1½-lb) onions, peeled and sliced
  (about 6 medium onions)
1 tablespoon sugar
50-ml (2-fl oz) Madeira
Grated cheese

Melt the butter in a frying pan. Add the onions and cook them over medium heat until they are soft and transparent.

Stir in the sugar, reduce the heat, and cook very slowly for about 1 hour. Stir in the wine, cook briefly, and pour over 450-g (1-lb) of freshly cooked pasta. Sprinkle with grated cheese.

MUSHROOM SAUCE

This makes a nice, quick sauce, even when you use cultivated mushrooms. But if you're fortunate enough to have some wild mushrooms on hand — morels, chanterelles, cèpes, even field mushrooms — you have a great experience in store for you.

ENOUGH FOR 225—350-g (½—¾-lb) PASTA
450-g (1-lb) mushrooms
100-g (4-oz) unsalted butter
3 shallots or small onions, minced or
  finely chopped
Salt and freshly ground black pepper
3 tablespoons chopped parsley

Wipe the mushrooms with a damp cloth and slice them lengthwise, through cap and stem. Melt the butter in a frying pan, add the mushrooms and shallots, and sauté them quickly over fairly high heat, tossing them in the pan and seasoning them as they cook with the salt and pepper. Pour over freshly cooked pasta, mix well, and sprinkle with chopped parsley.

HERBED BUTTER SAUCE

I like to make this sauce with tarragon, but if you have a special fondness for some other herb, or if you look on the shelf and there is no tarragon, by all means be flexible. Best

74

of all, of course, is a fresh herb, and I have the idea that more and more cooks are going back to growing their own herb gardens in their kitchen windows or small garden plots.

ENOUGH FOR ABOUT 225-g (½-lb) PASTA
225-g (8-oz) unsalted butter
1 shallot or small onion, finely chopped
1 teaspoon dried tarragon, or 2 tablespoons
  fresh tarragon
2 tablespoons chopped parsley
Few drops lemon juice

Melt the butter in a heavy pan, taking care not to let it brown. Skim off the white froth that rises to the top. Add the shallot and tarragon and sauté gently for about 3 minutes. Add the parsley and lemon juice, stir once, and pour the sauce over hot drained pasta.

PASTA PRIMAVERA

In Italian, *primavera* means 'spring', and a primavera sauce should be made with the first, tiny vegetables that pop out in the spring. In the winter, of course, you would use the freshest vegetables you could get at that time, such as broccoli, red peppers, and courgettes, but I've suggested a spring-time combination that would be delicious. Just don't be formal about it. Use what you have in the garden or in the refrigerator. You can even cut up a couple of stalks of celery and add them for the bite.

4 TO 6 SERVINGS
75-g (3-oz) fresh peas
75-g (3-oz) tiny, new beans
75-g (3-oz) sliced stalks thin asparagus
25—40-g (1—1½-oz) sliced mushrooms
50-g (2-oz) unsalted butter
225-ml (8-fl oz) single cream, warmed
Lots of freshly ground black pepper
450-g (1-lb) angel's hair, linguine, or even orzo
Grated Parmesan cheese

Lightly cook the peas, beans, asparagus, and mushrooms in the butter until everything is crisply tender. Add the cream and pepper and cook down briefly. Cook the pasta, drain it, and toss with the sauce. Sprinkle with lots of grated Parmesan cheese.

SAUTÉED VEGETABLES WITH SPÄTZLE

You can use any seasonal vegetables in this sauté, as long as you have an eye for colour. This is a good winter combination, with one white, one orange, and one green vegetable. It takes a lot of pepper.

4 TO 6 SERVINGS
1 recipe Spätzle (p. 55)
½ large turnip, in matchsticks
3 carrots, in matchsticks
3 small courgettes, in matchsticks
100-g (4-oz) unsalted butter
Salt and lots of freshly ground black pepper
15-g (½-oz) chopped parsley

Cook the spätzle. Rinse them under cold water and spread them to dry on a dinner plate. Steam the turnip and carrot strips over boiling water until they are just soft, crisp, and brightly coloured. Take them out, plunge them into cold water to stop the cooking, and drain them well. The courgettes do not have to be pre-cooked. All of this preparation can be done several hours before you make the sauté.

When you are ready to cook, melt the butter in a large frying pan. Toss the vegetables and spätzle in the hot butter until they are heated through. Do not let them become limp: they should retain their colour and stay crisply tender. Season with salt, a great deal of pepper, and the chopped parsley.

SPAGHETTINI WITH ASPARAGUS

You could try this with any fresh vegetable — peas, for instance, or broccoli — and you'd have an exciting meal. Oddly enough, the Worcestershire sauce doesn't overwhelm the delicate taste of the asparagus. You could use soy sauce, but the Worcestershire gives it a little extra push.

4 TO 6 SERVINGS
450-g (1-lb) asparagus, cut in thin diagonal strips
50-g (2-oz) butter
2 large cloves garlic, finely chopped
2 tablespoons lemon juice
1 tablespoon Worcestershire sauce
1 teaspoon freshly ground black pepper
450-g (1-lb) spaghettini

Heat a pan of water. When it is boiling furiously, drop in the asparagus pieces and cook for just 2 minutes. Pour them into a colander and refresh them under cold water.

Melt the butter in a large frying pan. Add the asparagus, garlic, lemon juice, Worcestershire sauce, and pepper. Toss everything well for a minute or two. Cook the spaghettini in boiling water. Drain and then combine with the asparagus.

FETTUCCINE WITH COURGETTES

A very pretty dish when it is made with yellow eggy noodles, green courgettes, and red pepper strips, like the Italian flag.

4 TO 6 SERVINGS
450-g (1-lb) small, firm courgettes
2 red peppers, peeled
100-ml (4-fl oz) olive oil
2 onions, chopped
2 cloves garlic, crushed
4 large tomatoes, peeled, seeded, and chopped,
* or one 450-g (16-oz) tin Italian plum tomatoes*
1 teaspoon salt
⅛ teaspoon dried red chili peppers, crumbled
450-g (1-lb) fettuccine

Trim the ends from the courgettes and slice them into julienne strips. Cut the peppers into strips. Heat the olive oil in a frying pan, and sauté the onions, garlic, courgettes, and peppers for 5 minutes, stirring occasionally. Add the tomatoes, salt, and dried chili peppers, and cook over very low heat for another 5 to 10 minutes.

Cook the fettuccine. Drain and pour the sauce over the hot pasta.

SPAGHETTINI WITH FRIED AUBERGINE

4 TO 6 SERVINGS
1 medium aubergine
1½ teaspoons salt
Vegetable oil (preferably peanut)
50-g (2-oz) flour
1 teaspoon freshly ground black pepper
2 eggs, lightly beaten
100-g (4-oz) fresh breadcrumbs

78

about 350-g (12-oz) Fresh Tomato Sauce
  (p. 72)
450-g (1-lb) spaghettini
at least 50-g (2-oz) grated Parmesan cheese

Cut the aubergine into 3-mm (⅛-inch) slices. Place in a bowl and sprinkle with 1 teaspoon salt. Weight the slices down with a plate and a 1.8-kg (4-lb) weight for 2 to 3 hours, draining off water as it accumulates. Rinse off the salt and dry on paper towels.

Pour 5-cm (2-inches) of the oil in a deep frying pan and heat to 185°C (360°F). Slice the aubergine across into 1-cm (½-inch) strips. Put the flour and pepper into a plastic bag and add the aubergine slices. Shake well to coat. Remove and dip in egg, then in crumbs, and fry in the hot oil until golden brown. Remove to paper towels.

Heat the tomato sauce. Cook the spaghettini. Drain and pour the sauce over the hot pasta. Serve topped with the fried aubergine strips and grated cheese.

PASTA ESTIVI

Some friends brought this recipe back from Italy. *Estivi* means 'summer', and it makes an elegant summer lunch, especially good on our basil-flavoured noodles (p. 48). Be sure that the pasta is very hot and the sauce icy-cold.

  2 TO 4 SERVINGS
  2 large ripe tomatoes, peeled and cut
    into sixths
  1 medium onion, peeled and sliced into rings
  4 tablespoons olive oil
  1 tablespoon white wine vinegar
  Lots of freshly ground black pepper
  225-g (8-oz) green noodles
  2 tablespoons chopped fresh basil, if available
  Chopped parsley

Mix the tomatoes, onion, olive oil, and vinegar. Sprinkle with lots of pepper, and let sit for at least an hour, to give the onions a chance to lose their sharpness.

Cook the pasta in boiling water, and drain. Spoon the cold sauce over the hot pasta, and sprinkle with fresh basil and parsley.

VARIATION
- Instead of the onion, use 4 sliced spring onions.

TURNIP GREENS WITH PINE KERNELS

The leaves of young turnips' tops are an unusual change from spring greens. You can substitute chard if turnip tops are not available.

2 SERVINGS
About 900-g (2-lb) turnip greens or chard
50-ml (2-fl oz) olive oil
1 fat clove garlic, peeled
225-g (8-oz) noodles
75-g (3-oz) pine kernels
¼ teaspoon salt

Wash the leaves and chop them coarsely. Heat the oil in a frying pan with the clove of garlic, taking care that the garlic doesn't burn. Add the leaves, cover the pan, and cook for about 5 minutes, until wilted. Shake the pan occasionally to stop them sticking.

Cook the pasta in boiling water, and drain it. Remove the cover from the leaves, add the pine kernels, and remove the garlic clove. Season with salt and pour over the freshly cooked noodles.

PASTA WITH PARSLEY PESTO

If you can't find cherry tomatoes — small, delicious, and tasty — use the smallest you can get hold of or, in extremis, halve larger ones (but the visual effect won't be the same).

4 TO 6 SERVINGS
4 to 5 bunches parsley, stems removed
3 large cloves garlic
100-g (4-oz) broken or split walnuts
225-ml (8-fl oz) olive oil
1 ½ teaspoons salt
at least 50-g (2-oz) grated Parmesan cheese
50-g (2-oz) unsalted butter
15-g (½-oz) chopped fresh dill
  or 1 tablespoon dried dill
450-g (1-lb) cherry tomatoes
450-g (1-lb) pasta
2 tablespoons olive oil

Combine the parsley, garlic, walnuts, olive oil, salt, and cheese in the beaker of a food processor. Process the ingredients until you have a well-blended pesto.

Melt the butter in the top of a double boiler over simmering water. Add the chopped dill and the tomatoes. Toss the tomatoes to coat with the dill butter and leave just long enough to heat through.

Cook and then toss the freshly cooked pasta with 2 tablespoons olive oil. Place a portion of the pasta on each plate with some of the pesto on top. Arrange the cherry tomatoes alongside the pasta and spoon some of the dill butter sauce over them. Serve at once.

NOODLES WITH CABBAGE

I made this up years ago, when I wanted something to serve with sausages and beer. Try it with wide egg noodles or noodle squares or tiny spätzle or nockerli.

6 TO 8 SERVINGS
One cabbage, about 1—1.3-kg (2—3-lb)
5 tablespoons bacon fat or 65-g (2½-oz) butter
2 tablespoons flour
175-ml (6-fl oz) single cream
Salt and freshly ground black pepper
450-g (1-lb) noodles or dumplings

Put the cabbage through the slicing blade of the food processor. Melt the butter or bacon fat in a large frying pan and sauté the cabbage until it is lightly browned. Cover and cook for 10 minutes. Sprinkle on the flour and continue to cook, stirring for a few minutes. Then add the cream, salt, and pepper, and cook, stirring constantly, until the sauce is thickened.

Cook the noodles or dumplings. Drain them, add them to the pot, and let everything bubble together for a few minutes to blend the flavours.

VEGETABLE–NOODLE CASSEROLE

An old-fashioned American dish, despite the tomatoes, courgettes, oregano, and garlic. It was just the thing to take along to a covered-dish supper or to serve to the family for Sunday supper.

6 TO 8 SERVINGS
50-g (2-oz) butter
2 tablespoons olive oil
3 onions, sliced

1 clove garlic, chopped
50-g (2-oz) finely chopped parsley
¼ teaspoon dried oregano
4 tomatoes, peeled, seeded, and chopped
225-ml (8-fl oz) chicken stock
Salt and freshly ground black pepper
450-g (1-lb) wide noodles
3 small, firm courgettes, sliced
Grated Cheddar or Gruyère cheese

Melt half the butter and the oil in a heavy saucepan. Add the onions, garlic, parsley, and oregano, and cook, stirring occasionally, until the onions are golden. Add the tomatoes and chicken stock, salt, and pepper, and cook for 10 minutes.

Cook and drain the noodles. Mix the rest of the butter with the freshly cooked noodles. Stir in the tomato sauce and the courgette slices and pour the mixture into a buttered baking dish. Sprinkle the top with a handful of grated cheese, dot with more butter, and bake for 15 to 20 minutes at 190°C (375°F), Gas 5.

PASTA WITH BEANS

This is the heartiest dish imaginable, just the thing for a cold winter night. It's one of those unrefined peasant dishes that deliver a lot of taste, satisfaction, and protein for relatively little cost. Serve with good bread and a simple strong red wine.

6 TO 8 SERVINGS

450-g (1-lb) dried white haricot beans, or
  one 450-g (16-oz) tin white beans
50-ml (2-fl oz) olive oil
100-g (4-oz) streaky bacon, in 2.5-cm
  (1-inch) strips
2 onions, chopped
2 carrots, chopped
50-g (2-oz) finely chopped parsley
1 teaspoon dried oregano
2 tablespoons dried basil
450-g (16-oz) tin Italian plum tomatoes, or
  4 large tomatoes, peeled, seeded, and chopped
100-ml (4-fl oz) bean liquid
2 teaspoons salt
1 teaspoon freshly ground black pepper
450-g (1-lb) elbow macaroni (tubetti lunghi)
50-g (2-oz) butter, at room temperature
50-g (2-oz) grated sharp cheese
Chopped parsley

If you use dried beans, cover them with cold water, bring to the boil, cook 2 minutes, and then remove from the heat and let stand, covered, for 1 hour. If you use canned beans, merely drain them and set them aside, reserving 100-ml (4-fl oz) of the liquid.

Continue cooking the beans over medium heat till they are just tender. Drain. Reserve some of the liquid for the sauce.

Heat the olive oil in a heavy casserole and sauté the bacon strips until they are half cooked. Add the onions, carrots, parsley, oregano, and basil, and cook until the vegetables have wilted. Add the tomatoes, bean liquid, salt, and pepper. Cover and simmer for about 10 minutes, until the vegetables are tender. Add the drained cooked beans and simmer for another 20 minutes.

Meanwhile cook and drain the macaroni. Toss with bits of

the butter and grated cheese, and then mix with the bean sauce and a little of the bean liquid. Serve in heated bowls, and sprinkle more cheese and chopped parsley on the top.

AVOCADO PASTA

This is a superb dish, but it's a bit tricky to handle because of the softness of the dough. You could make only the avocado sauce, and use commercial spinach pasta for the colour, but it wouldn't have the delicate sensuous flavour of the real thing.

6 TO 8 SERVINGS
400-g (14-oz) flour
¼ teaspoon salt
3 very ripe avocados
3 eggs
25-g (1-oz) butter
1 clove garlic, crushed
½ teaspoon salt
½ teaspoon freshly ground black pepper
450-ml (16-fl oz) double cream
3 tablespoons grated Parmesan cheese
Pickled red pepper or pimiento

To make the pasta, put the flour and ¼ teaspoon salt in a large mixing bowl. In another bowl, mash one of the avocados, which you have first peeled and cut into chunks. Stir in the eggs with a wooden spoon. Add the avocado mixture to the flour and blend thoroughly in the bowl or in the food processor.

Turn out the dough onto a floured board and knead it by hand for 5 minutes. The avocado will have made it very soft, so that you will have to sprinkle it frequently with more flour. Roll it into very thin sheets, using the machine. Cut the sheets into 3.75-cm (1½-inch) squares. Lay them on a baking tray or a piece of foil and chill them in the freezer for about a half hour, until they are firm.

Bring a large pan of salted water to the boil. When the dough squares are firm, take them out of the freezer, drop them into the boiling water, and cook for about 3 minutes, until they are properly done. Drain. Return the pasta to the pan, and add the butter, garlic, salt, pepper, cream, and the remaining 2 avocados, peeled and cubed. Sprinkle with Parmesan cheese and stir gently over medium heat so that everything is coated. Transfer to a serving dish, sprinkle with more cheese, and serve at once, garnished with slivers of red pimiento.

FISH AND SEAFOOD

ANGEL'S HAIR WITH GOLDEN-RED CAVIAR

SPAGHETTI WITH CLAM SAUCE
(with mussels or oysters)

LINGUINE WITH TOMATO-SHRIMP SAUCE
(with scallops · tuna · squid · or mussels)

FETTUCCINE WITH SEA BASS
(with flounder or other flat fish)

SCALLOPS PROVENÇALE OVER SPAGHETTINI

SWORDFISH-OLIVE PASTA

PASTA WITH SARDINES

ANGEL'S HAIR WITH GOLDEN-RED CAVIAR

This is one of the most elegant dishes in the book, and yet it's made in moments. The golden-red American salmon roe has larger eggs than those in *real* caviar (or in the less real lumpfish roe), costs far less than other varieties, and can even be stored in the freezer. Or pressed caviar can be used instead. It's absolutely delicious, and a stunning appetiser.

4 SERVINGS
225-g (8-oz) angel's hair pasta
350-g (12-oz) unsalted butter, at room temperature
200-g (7-oz) salmon roe or pressed caviar
4 thin lemon wedges

Cook and drain the pasta. Put it into a warmed bowl with the butter. Toss well, until all the pasta is coated with butter, and then put a serving on each plate. Top each with a heaping tablespoonful of caviar and a lemon wedge. Each person should squeeze lemon juice over the noodles before he mixes in the caviar.

Champagne or iced vodka accompany this admirably. Don't stint on the caviar if possible!

SPAGHETTI WITH CLAM SAUCE

I discovered this wonderfully light sauce, full of the essence of clams and garlic, during one of those periods when I was seriously trying to cut down on oil and salt. I don't think you miss the oil at all.

If you can't get hold of fresh clams, use two 300-g (10-oz) tins baby clams in brine. Simmer the stock for 10 minutes, drain the clams, and heat them through in the hot stock for no more than 1 minute. Proceed as below.

4 TO 6 SERVINGS
about 2 litres (3¼-pt) small clams (little neck or
cherry stone)

White wine
4 to 5 large cloves garlic, minced or crushed
450-g (1-lb) spaghetti
40-g (1½-oz) chopped parsley

Scrub the clams well and wash them in cold water to remove the sand in the shells. Put them in a heavy saucepan with about 1-cm (½-inch) of white wine or water and the garlic. Cover tightly, and steam the clams until the shells open, from 5 to 10 minutes. Discard any that have not opened.

Cook and drain the pasta. Put the freshly cooked spaghetti in a warm bowl, pour the clams, still in their shells, and stock over it, and sprinkle parsley on the top.

VARIATIONS

• Instead of clams, you can use the same quantity of mussels or oysters. If you use mussels, scrub them well with a scouring pad, scrape off the encrustations on the shells, and snip off the beards before you steam them.

LINGUINE WITH TOMATO–SHRIMP SAUCE

Make this mixture as hot as you like by adding a good dash of Tabasco or red chili-pepper flakes. For me, the hotter the better.

4 TO 6 SERVINGS
1 recipe Light Tomato Sauce (p. 71), without
    the butter
225-g (8-oz) peeled raw shrimps or prawns
2 cloves garlic, finely chopped
3 tablespoons chopped flat-leaved parsley
2 tablespoons olive oil
Tabasco or red chili-pepper flakes, to taste
450-g (1-lb) linguine

91

Cook the sauce. When it is finished, add the shrimps or prawns, garlic, parsley, olive oil, and Tabasco or chili. Simmer for 3 minutes.

Cook and drain the linguine, and serve with the hot sauce.

VARIATIONS

- Instead of shrimps, use 225-g (8-oz) scallops out of their shells cut in quarters; one 200-g (7-oz) tin tuna; 225-g (½-lb) squid, sliced into rings; or 18 mussels. If you use the mussels, simmer the sauce, covered, just until the shells open, around 8 to 10 minutes, and keep the pepper seasoning mild.

FETTUCCINE WITH SEA BASS

This is a richly flavoured, substantial dish that has the spring-time flavour of fresh herbs. Most markets have fresh dill all year round these days, but if you want a real treat, make it with chives instead. I'd like to encourage cooks to go back to the old custom of keeping flowerpots of fresh chives growing in their kitchen windows.

> 4 TO 6 SERVINGS
> *50-g (2-oz) butter*
> *1 tablespoon olive oil*
> *225-g (8-oz) bass (bar or loup de mer) fillets,*
> * or more, if wanted*
> *100-ml (4-fl oz) cream*
> *Salt and freshly ground black pepper*
> *450-g (1-lb) fettuccine*
> *at least 25-g (1-oz) finely chopped dill or chives*

In a frying pan, melt the butter and olive oil. When they are hot, add the fish and cook it on both sides until cooked through, about 5 minutes, depending on the thickness of the fish. Flake the fish with a fork straight into the butter, then add the cream and let it cook down briefly. Season with salt and pepper.

Cook and drain the pasta. Pour the sauce over the freshly cooked noodles, and scatter lots and lots of dill or chives over the top before you toss everything together.

VARIATIONS
- Fillets of flounder or other flat fish, such as lemon sole or plaice, will be a most welcome substitute for the bass. Probably they will be thinner and most likely will cook in less time.

SCALLOPS PROVENÇALE OVER SPAGHETTINI

Tiny bay or 'queen' scallops, if you can get them, should be cooked very briefly, or they become tough, so have everything ready when you make this dish and be prepared to work quickly. The pasta must be cooked before you start to sauté the scallops. It's a nice touch to add a splash of Cognac for quality just at the end.

> 4 TO 6 SERVINGS
> *450-g (1-lb) tiny shelled scallops, or 8—12 larger*
>   *scallops, shelled and thickly sliced*
> *2 tablespoons flour*
> *450-g (1-lb) spaghettini*
> *150-ml (5-fl oz) olive oil*
> *3 or 4 cloves garlic, finely chopped*
> *50-g (1-oz) finely chopped parsley*
> *Lots of freshly ground black pepper*
> *2 tablespoons Cognac*

Bring the pasta water to a boil.

Toss the whole scallops or scallop slices in the flour so that they are lightly coated. Drop the pasta into a pot to cook. Quickly heat the oil in a good non-stick frying pan and, when it is hot, throw in the scallops and toss like mad. Shake and stir the pan for not more than 2 minutes.

Off heat add the garlic, parsley, and pepper to the scallops and toss for another minute. Pour in the Cognac and cook for another half minute.

Drain the pasta and pour the sauce over it.

SWORDFISH–OLIVE PASTA

I like to use twists, shells, or ridged ziti for this dish: something that will catch all the tangy bits of olive and capers. What you want is the rich, exciting olive taste, so use lots and lots of finely chopped Greek olives.

Swordfish is occasionally sold in good fishmongers in Britain, although it is widely available on the Continent. Tuna steaks, or occasionally shark or dolphin steaks, might be a substitute.

2 TO 4 SERVINGS
225-g (8-oz) swordfish (2.5-cm or 1-inch thick)
at least 150-g (5-oz) finely chopped Greek olives
50-ml (2-fl oz) olive oil
125—150-g (4—5-oz) thinly sliced onion
2 large cloves garlic, finely chopped
1 teaspoon dried oregano
1 tablespoon capers
225-g (8-oz) pasta

Pre-heat the grill and line the rack with aluminium foil. Grill the swordfish 3 minutes on one side, turn, top with the olives, and grill 4 minutes longer. In the meantime, pour the oil into a frying pan and cook the onion and garlic until they are soft. Add the oregano and capers.

Cook and drain the pasta.

When the fish is cooked, remove it from the grill and cut into thin strips. Spoon it and the olives, with the onion-caper mixture, over freshly cooked pasta and toss gently.

PASTA WITH SARDINES

This recipe is a big hit whenever I teach it in one of my classes. The original called for fresh sardines, but smelts can be used too. See if you can get your fish dealer to clean and bone them for you; if not, you'll have to do it yourself. You can use tinned sardines, but they are definitely second best. Drain, rinse, and handle them very carefully or they'll flake away to a paste.

6 TO 8 SERVINGS
2 fennel bulbs
50-ml (2-fl oz) olive oil
1 large onion, chopped
450-g (16-oz) tin Italian plum tomatoes, or
    5 fresh salad tomatoes, peeled, seeded,
    and chopped
75-g (3-oz) raisins
150-g (5-oz) pine kernels
¼ teaspoon powdered saffron
½ teaspoon dried basil
1 tin anchovy fillets, drained, rinsed,
    and chopped
450-g (1-lb) sardines or smelts, cleaned and
    boned (If you have any really tiny fish,
    leave some whole and treat according to
    the directions in the recipe below.)
450-g (1-lb) pasta, such as penne or macaroni
Salt and freshly ground black pepper

Cut off and discard the fennel tops and cut the bulbs into very thin, lengthwise slices. Cook them in a big pot of boiling water until they are tender, about 5 minutes. Skim them out with a slotted spoon, set them aside, and leave the water at a simmer for when you cook the pasta.

Heat the olive oil in a large frying pan and sauté the onion until it is soft. Add the tomatoes, raisins, pine kernels, saffron, basil, anchovies, and sardines, and cook for another

10 minutes. If you have any very small smelts, reserve them whole. Coat them with some flour, sauté them in another pan in olive oil until they are brown and crisp, drain them on paper towels, and keep in a warm oven until you are ready to use them.

Turn up the heat under your simmering water. Add the pasta and cook until it is done. Just before you pour it out, return the fennel to the pot to reheat it. Drain the pasta and fennel and pour them into a warmed bowl. Add salt and pepper to taste. Pour on the tomato sauce and mix everything together. If you have whole fried smelts, lay them on top of the sauce.

MEATS

PENNE OR ZITI WITH TOMATO-MEAT SAUCE
(with shrimps or prawns · with clams ·
with mussels)

VERNA ROSS'S BAKED CHICKEN GOULASH
AND SPAGHETTI

OLD-FASHIONED CHICKEN FRICASSEE
WITH PASTA WHEELS

CHICKEN TETRAZZINI
(with curry · with truffle and almonds)

NUTTED CHICKEN-RICE NOODLE CASSEROLE

CHICKEN POT PIE

COQ AU RIESLING OVER NOODLES
(with guinea fowl · with game birds)

CHICKEN STIR-FRY WITH FARFALLI

PASTA-STUFFED ROAST CHICKEN

PASTA AND GIBLETS

PASTA WITH CHICKEN LIVER AND ARTICHOKE SAUCE

GRILLED DUCK WITH RICE NOODLES

PEKING CURRY-TOMATO SAUCE ON NOODLES

PASTITSIO FOR A PARTY

LEON LIANIDES'S LEG OF LAMB WITH ORZO

BEEF AND SCALLOPS
WITH CELLOPHANE NOODLES

BEACH PÂTÉ

CHILI SHORT RIBS AND MACARONI

LASAGNE

SAVOURY TONGUE WITH FINE NOODLES

OSSI BUCHI WITH ORZO

SAUSAGE-TOMATO SAUCE OVER PENNE

PORK WITH SAUERKRAUT NOODLES

SOFT NOODLES SAUTÉED

TAGLIARINI VERDI AL GUANCIALE

GNOCCHI À LA PARISIENNE

PENNE OR ZITI WITH TOMATO–MEAT SAUCE

This is a good scheme to follow whenever you have some leftover meat in the refrigerator. It's delicious made with chicken, beef, pork, veal, even brains. The seasoning will depend on whatever your meat was seasoned with when it was first cooked. If you have some meat juices left from underneath a roast or from a sauté pan, by all means add them to the sauce, too. And, if you don't, and have a delicate meat such as chicken or veal, add 50-ml (2-fl oz) cream to the sauce at the end. A wonderful way to use leftovers — let your imagination guide you!

> 6 TO 8 SERVINGS
> *1 recipe Light Tomato Sauce (p. 71)*
> *275-g (10-oz) minced cooked meat*
> *Pan juices or 50-ml (2-fl oz) cream (optional)*
> *450-g (1-lb) penne or ziti*

Make the sauce. When it is done, add the minced cooked meat and the pan juices or cream. Season to taste, and simmer for 5 minutes while you cook the pasta. Drain, and serve the sauce over the hot pasta.

VARIATIONS

● Substitute 225-g (8-oz) or more cooked shrimps or prawns for the meat. Add a touch more pepper and 50—75-g (2—3-oz) finely chopped red or green peppers.

● Steam clams as described on page 91. Remove from shell and add clam stock and clams to tomato sauce. Combine with pasta. No cheese! (Or use tins of baby clams.)

● You may do the same with mussels as with the clams. Remove shell before adding to pasta.

VERNA ROSS'S BAKED CHICKEN GOULASH AND SPAGHETTI

This is a very homely dish that I used to eat a great deal in the West. There was a time when everyone was making it. I think of it as very American, one of those things you can carry to a picnic or to a big buffet party. It's quite unsophisticated, but it tastes just fine.

12 TO 14 SERVINGS
1.8—2-kg (4—5-lb) chicken or capon, boiled
  and cooled
4—5 onions, chopped
50-g (2-oz) butter
450-g (1-lb) fresh mushrooms
900-g (2-lb) spaghetti
1 tin whole-kernel sweetcorn, or
  1 packet frozen sweetcorn
800-g (28-oz) tin tomatoes
450-g (1-lb) packet frozen peas
225-g (8-oz) grated mild Cheddar cheese

Remove the meat from the chicken and pull it apart into fairly large pieces.

Sauté the onions in the butter until just lightly cooked. Add the mushrooms and sauté a few minutes more.

Meanwhile cook the spaghetti in the stock in which the chicken was cooked. Mix the meat with the drained cooked spaghetti. Add the sweetcorn, onions, tomatoes, peas, and mushrooms, and turn the whole mixture into a large casserole. Cover the top with grated cheese, and bake in a 180°C (350°F), Gas 4 oven for 45 minutes.

OLD-FASHIONED CHICKEN FRICASSEE
WITH PASTA WHEELS

A wonderfully soothing dish, a great old favourite. If your family likes only the white or only the dark meat, you can buy your chicken in pieces instead of whole, and no one will feel disappointed. Wide noodles are traditional, but I served a fricassee with pasta wheels recently, and it made an amusing change.

6 SERVINGS
50-g (2-oz) unsalted butter
1.6—1.8-kg (3½—4-lb) chicken or capon
   cut in pieces
about 150-g (5-oz) sliced celery
150-g (5-oz) finely chopped onions
2 tablespoons finely chopped shallots
2 tablespoons flour
350-ml (12-fl oz) chicken stock
225-ml (8-fl oz) double cream
1 teaspoon salt
Freshly ground black pepper
Pinch of cayenne pepper
⅛ teaspoon nutmeg
2 egg yolks
2 teaspoons fresh lemon juice
450-g (1-lb) wheels or other pasta

Melt half the butter in a large frying pan with a lid. When the foam subsides, add the chicken to the pan and cook it for 1 minute, until it becomes firm on the outside but has not yet browned. Turn and seal the other side, and remove the chicken from the pan.

Melt the remaining butter in the pan. When it is bubbling, stir in the celery, onions, and shallots. When they are nicely coated with butter, sprinkle on the flour and cook it briefly, stirring all the time. Do not let it brown. Add the chicken stock gradually, whisking constantly to avoid lumps.

Return the chicken to the pan with half the cream, salt, pepper, cayenne, and nutmeg. Shake the pan to blend the spices. Bring the sauce to a low simmer, put the cover in place, and lower the heat. Cook over low heat for 20 minutes.

Take the lid off and remove the chicken to a covered dish, putting it in a 120°C (250°F), Gas ½ oven to keep it warm. Tip the pan and, using a flat spoon, skim off the surface fat from the sauce.

In a small bowl, whisk together the remaining cream and the egg yolks. Slowly pour about 225-ml (8-fl oz) of the hot sauce into the egg mixture in a thin stream while you continue to whisk it. Then return the egg-sauce mixture to the pan containing the hot sauce. Cook it over low heat until it thickens to a light, creamy consistency that just coats the spoon. It must not overheat or begin to simmer, or it may curdle. Season with lemon juice and with more salt, if necessary.

Cook the pasta. Drain it, and combine with some of the sauce. Make a bed of pasta on a platter, and lay the chicken pieces on it, coated with the sauce.

CHICKEN TETRAZZINI

Despite its Italian name, this is an all-American dish, probably invented in San Francisco to honour a famous singer. Now we remember her because of this dish. The whole point is in the chicken stock; if you have a good, rich stock, your sauce will be properly flavoured. If it's good it's marvellous, if bad — a mess.

6 TO 8 SERVINGS
1.6—1.8-kg (3½—4-lb) chicken, cooked
2 red peppers, peeled
75-g (3-oz) unsalted butter
6 tablespoons flour
600-ml (1-pt) good chicken stock
225-ml (8-fl oz) double cream
Salt and freshly ground black pepper
¼ teaspoon Tabasco
100-ml (4-fl oz) sherry
450-g (1-lb) spaghetti
50-g (2-oz) soft white breadcrumbs
40-g (1½-oz) grated Parmesan cheese

Remove the meat from the chicken and set it aside. Cut the peppers into dice. To make a velouté sauce, melt the butter in a heavy saucepan, then stir in the flour. When it is cooked and bubbling, stir in the chicken stock gradually, continuing to stir until the sauce is thickened. Add the cream, and season with the salt, pepper, Tabasco, and sherry.

Put the chicken and diced peppers into the sauce, and hold over low heat while you cook and drain the spaghetti and arrange it in a buttered baking dish. Spoon the chicken and sauce over the spaghetti. Cover the top with the breadcrumbs and Parmesan cheese and dot with butter. Place in a 240°C (475°F), Gas 9 oven for a few minutes until the topping is glazed and bubbling.

VARIATIONS

● To make a lightly curried Tetrazzini, add 1 tablespoon or more curry powder to the butter when you first make the velouté. Let it cook for a minute before you add the flour.

● If you are feeling rich and elegant, add a finely chopped black truffle to the chicken. Instead of a mixture of crumbs and cheese sprinkle toasted sliced almonds over the top.

NUTTED CHICKEN–RICE NOODLE CASSEROLE

I first had this in a Danish restaurant in Seattle at least forty years ago, and I just loved the crust of buttery, crunchy sliced almonds. I suppose we should offer it to some prima donna, because it's very much like Chicken Tetrazzini. Perhaps, in honour of its origin, we should call it Chicken Nilsson.

6 SERVINGS
225-g (8-oz) rice noodles, sticks or vermicelli
40—50-g (1½—2-oz) unsalted butter
3 tablespoons flour
450-ml (16-fl oz) good chicken stock
100-ml (4-fl oz) double cream
2 tablespoons Cognac
1½ teaspoons salt
½ teaspoon freshly ground black pepper
1 teaspoon dried tarragon
Dash of Tabasco
*675-g (1½-lb) poached chicken, removed from
   the bone*
75-g (3-oz) sliced almonds, toasted

Cover the noodles with cold water, and let them soak for 3 to 4 hours. (But follow the instructions on the packet.) If you use ordinary wheat noodles, cook them in boiling water, drain, and set them aside.

To make the sauce, melt the butter in a heavy-bottomed pan. Mix the flour into the melted butter and cook it slowly, stirring all the time, for 2 to 3 minutes, until the roux is well blended. Stir in the chicken stock and cook until the sauce is smooth, thick and at boiling point. Add the cream, Cognac, salt, pepper, tarragon, and Tabasco, and cook briefly to heat through and blend the flavours. An additional 15-g (½-oz) of butter swirled in at this point will give an even richer sauce. Add the chicken to the pan, taste, and correct the seasoning.

Arrange the noodles in a buttered baking dish. Spoon the chicken mixture evenly over them, and cover the chicken with a good layer of toasted almonds. Dot with butter. Bake in a 180°C (350°F), Gas 4 oven for 20 minutes, when the top should be brown and crunchy, an absolutely delicious finish.

CHICKEN POT PIE

Not at all what you think it is. In Pennsylvania Dutch cooking, 'pot pies' are noodle squares that are added to rich chicken or beef stock. You serve them in a bowl, with a lot of stock and some of the chicken.

6 TO 8 SERVINGS
1.8—2.2-kg (4—5-lb) boiling fowl or roasting
  chicken or capon
1 leek, washed and trimmed
1 onion, peeled and stuck with 1 clove
1 carrot, scraped
1 clove garlic, peeled
1 bay leaf
2 sprigs parsley
3 peppercorns
Salt

NOODLES:
300-g (10-oz) flour
2 eggs
15-g (½-oz) butter or chicken fat
½ teaspoon salt

Chopped parsley

Put the chicken in a large pan with the leek, onion, carrot, garlic, bay leaf, parsley, and peppercorns. Barely cover with water (or, for a richer taste, with chicken stock). Bring the liquid slowly to a boil and reduce the heat, skimming off any scum that rises to the surface. Cover the pot and simmer very gently, so that the surface barely moves, for about 1 hour for a young chicken and 2 or more hours for a boiling fowl. Transfer the chicken to a platter and, when it is cool enough to handle, take off the skin, pull the meat from the bones, and cut it into large pieces. Strain the stock, correct the seasoning, and put it back on the stove while you make the pot pies.

To make the noodles: combine the flour, eggs, butter or chicken fat, and salt with enough water to make a stiff dough — about 100-ml (4-fl oz). Make them as you would any noodles — by hand, in the mixer, or in the food processor. Let rest, knead, and let rest again. Roll out the dough on a floured board or through the smooth wheels of the pasta machine. With a knife or pastry wheel, cut the dough into 5-cm (2-inch) squares. Use them immediately or dry them as you would any other noodles. When you are ready to serve the pot pies, return the chicken pieces to the stock and simmer for a few minutes to heat through. Then lay the noodle squares in the simmering stock and cook them for about 15 minutes. Ladle stock, chicken, and pot pies into soup bowls, and sprinkle with lots of parsley.

COQ AU RIESLING OVER NOODLES

This Alsatian speciality is a lighter, more delicate version of the Burgundian coq au vin. Any white wine will do, but for authenticity's sake you should try to get a slightly sweet Alsatian Riesling. Noodles, of course, are important in Alsatian cooking, having entered with the German influence.

6 TO 8 SERVINGS
50-g (2-oz) butter
2 tablespoons oil
Flour
8 chicken drumsticks and thighs
100-g (4-oz) salt pork, finely diced
450-g (1-lb) mushrooms
8 shallots or button onions, finely chopped
24 small button or pickling onions, peeled
3 carrots, cleaned and sliced
100-ml (4-fl oz) Cognac
Salt and freshly ground black pepper
2 cloves garlic, crushed
225-ml (16-fl oz) white wine
450-g (1-lb) fine Continental egg noodles
Chopped parsley

Heat the butter and oil in a heavy frying pan. Lightly flour the chicken pieces and brown them over medium-high heat, a few at a time, removing them to a large casserole as they are browned. In the fat remaining in the frying pan, render the salt pork by cooking it until the fat has melted and the pieces of pork are brown and crisp. Add the mushrooms, chopped onion or shallots, whole onions, and carrots and toss them in the fat until they are lightly browned. Add them to the chicken pieces in the casserole.

In a small saucepan, heat the Cognac. Pour it over the chicken and vegetables and set it alight. Baste the chicken with the blazing Cognac until the flames have died down, and season with salt, pepper, and garlic. Add the wine and simmer, covered, for 20 minutes. If the sauce seems too thin, thicken it with a beurre manié made of equal parts of butter and flour worked together with a fork and then dropped, bit by bit, into the simmering sauce.

Cook and drain the noodles. Make a bed of the cooked noodles on a heated platter. Arrange the chicken and vegetables on them, spoon on the sauce, and sprinkle everything with chopped parsley.

VARIATIONS
- If they are available, cut up 2 guinea fowl. Test for tenderness. Follow the rule for the chicken.
- Several kinds of game birds may be prepared the same way, although the cooking time will be longer. Grouse, partridge or pheasant should be cut in half, allowing one half per person. Allow 1 pigeon per person. Cook until tender, after browning in the frying pan. Quail will take less time but they are most satisfactory in flavour. Allow at least 2 per person. Watch them very carefully lest they overcook.

CHICKEN STIR-FRY WITH FARFALLI

This is a dish that tastes even better when you eat it cold the day after it is served. It's a mad combination of Italian, Chinese, and American foods, and it's just delicious.

4 SERVINGS
1 large or 2 small chicken breasts, boned
3 Italian sausages
Giblets, heart, and liver of a
  chicken (optional)
175-ml (6-fl oz) olive oil
3 medium onions, chopped
2 carrots, grated
1 large clove garlic, chopped
550-g (1¼-lb) Light Tomato Sauce (p. 71).
1 teaspoon Chinese 5-spice powder
1 teaspoon salt
1 teaspoon freshly ground black pepper
¼ teaspoon Tabasco
about 50-g (2-oz) chopped parsley
225-g (8-oz) bows or butterflies (farfalli)

Cut the chicken breasts into 2.5-cm (1-inch) cubes. Cover the sausages, and the chicken giblets, if you use them, with water, and poach for 5 minutes. Take them out of the water, cut the sausages into 1-cm (½-inch) slices and chop the giblets.

Heat the oil in a heavy 30-cm (12-inch) frying pan. Add the onions, carrots, and garlic, and stir-fry briskly for 1 minute. Add the chicken cubes, sausage slices, and chopped giblets, and stir-fry for 5 minutes more. Add the tomato sauce, 5-spice powder, salt, pepper, and Tabasco. Blend and simmer for 3 minutes. At the end, mix in the chopped parsley.

Cook and drain the pasta, add the drained pasta to the pan, and toss everything together well.

PASTA–STUFFED ROAST CHICKEN

This is as good a roast chicken as I've ever had, and I am a fanatic about roast chicken. When it's done at a high temperature, the bird stays tender and juicy, while the skin turns beautifully crisp. The stuffing was made with an interesting Italian double-elbow macaroni, but you could use plain elbows, penne, or twists instead.

> 4 SERVINGS
> *175-g (6-oz) pasta*
> *2 small bunches spring onions, sliced*
> *25—40-g (1—1½-oz) chopped flat-leaved parsley*
> *2 tablespoons pine kernels*
> *175-g (6-oz) Pesto (p. 70)*
> *1.8—2.2-kg (4—5-lb) roasting chicken or capon*
> *25-g (1-oz) butter*
> *4 rashers streaky bacon*

Cook and drain the pasta. Combine the pasta, spring onions, parsley, pine kernels, and pesto in a mixing bowl. Stuff the chicken with the mixture and close the opening by placing a slice of bread over it. Truss the chicken and rub it lightly with the butter.

Place the bird on its side on a rack in a shallow roasting tin. Cover with the bacon. Roast for 25 minutes at 220°C (425°F), Gas 7. Remove the bacon, turn the bird onto its other side, and cover with the same bacon rashers. Roast another 25 minutes. Place the chicken breast up, and discard the bacon. Roast for 20 to 25 minutes longer, basting with the pan juices.

At this point, if the thigh joint moves easily — if you can 'shake hands with the bird' — it's too late, the chicken is overcooked and dry! A better test is to insert a meat thermometer into the thigh, avoiding the bone. It should register 77°C (170°F) when the bird is done. Take it out of the oven, place it on a hot platter, and let it sit for a few minutes before you carve it.

PASTA AND GIBLETS

The lowly innards of a chicken have a wonderful taste and texture when they are cooked properly. This thrifty sauce has the surprisingly Chinese tastes of soy, sesame, and coriander.

6 TO 8 SERVINGS
675 g (1½ lb) chicken giblets and hearts
1 medium onion, chopped
50-ml (2-fl oz) oil
2 large cloves garlic, crushed
125—150-g (4—5-oz) spring onions, thinly sliced
25-g (1-oz) chopped fresh coriander leaves
50-g (2-oz) chopped parsley
2 tablespoons soy sauce
1 tablespoon Oriental sesame-seed oil
450-g (1-lb) Chinese egg noodles

111

Clean and trim the giblets. Parboil them for 30 to 40 minutes, until they are tender, and then cut them into thin slices. Sauté the onion in the oil until it is transparent. Add the giblets, garlic, and spring onions, and sauté them for 20 minutes, stirring occasionally. Season with the coriander, parsley, soy sauce, and sesame oil, and toss the mixture until it is well mixed and heated through.

Cook and drain the noodles, and serve with the sauce.

PASTA WITH CHICKEN LIVER AND ARTICHOKE SAUCE

This rather old-fashioned sauce is lightly thickened with flour. Despite the tomatoes, garlic, olive oil, and oregano, it's not Italian in feeling, and I wouldn't be surprised if it had originated in America. You might do it with some kind of long, flat noodles, or maybe with twists.

6 TO 8 SERVINGS
50-g (2-oz) butter
3 onions, chopped
3 tablespoons flour
450-ml (16-fl oz) chicken stock
450-g (16-oz) tin Italian plum tomatoes
1 teaspoon dried oregano
2 teaspoons salt
½ teaspoon freshly ground black pepper
50-ml (2-fl oz) olive oil
2 cloves garlic, crushed
225-g (8-oz) mushrooms, sliced
8 tinned artichoke hearts
225-g (8-oz) chicken livers, trimmed
450-g (1-lb) pasta
100-g (4-oz) grated cheese

Melt the butter in a saucepan, and cook the onions until they are transparent. Stir in the flour, and cook it gently over medium heat until the roux is golden and bubbling. Add the chicken stock and cook, stirring constantly, until thickened and smooth. Add the tomatoes, oregano, and half the salt and pepper. Cover and cook gently over low heat for 1 hour.

Heat the olive oil in a frying pan. Add the garlic, mushrooms, and artichokes, and sauté gently for 5 minutes, stirring frequently. Add the livers, raise the heat, and toss and turn them over high heat until they are well browned. Do not overcook, or they will toughen. Season with the rest of the salt and pepper, and pour into the tomato sauce.

Cook and drain the pasta. Pour the sauce over the freshly cooked pasta, sprinkle with cheese, and serve.

GRILLED DUCK WITH RICE NOODLES

This is a nice mixture of flavours, but you can use your imagination when you choose vegetables for the stir-fry. I can see putting in some watercress, for example, or some slender new asparagus. The crisply fried rice noodles are fun. People think they have to fry them a long time, but that's not the way to do it. You break them up, drop them in hot fat, and pull them right out. They take one minute, and you keep going until they are all nice and crispy. And excellent they are!

4 SERVINGS

225-g (8-oz) rice noodles or sticks
1 large duck or 2 small ducks
1 onion
1 stalk celery
2 teaspoons freshly ground black pepper
2 tablespoons soy sauce
Peanut oil
Plum sauce (available in Chinese grocers)
100-g (4-oz) mange-touts, sliced on the diagonal
2 bunches spring onions, sliced on the diagonal
100-g (4-oz) bean sprouts
125—150-g (4—5-oz) sliced celery
50-g (2-oz) dried mushrooms, Chinese or
  Italian, soaked and rinsed
2 tablespoons Worcestershire sauce

Soak the rice noodles in cold water for 3 to 4 hours. Remove the breast halves from the duck and set them aside on a grill rack.

Put the rest of the duck into a pan with the onion, celery stalk, 1 teaspoon pepper, and enough water to cover it. Bring to the boil, reduce the heat, and simmer for 1½ hours. Remove the duck from the stock and, when it is cool enough to handle, remove the legs and set them on the grill rack with the breasts. Skim the fat from the stock, bring it to the boil again, and cook it way down, until it is reduced to about 225-ml (8-fl oz). Blend in the soy sauce and set it over very low heat.

Brush the duck breast and legs with peanut oil and plum sauce. Place them under a preheated grill and cook for 5 minutes, turning half way through the cooking time. The breast meat will be quite rare. You can, of course, cook it longer, but it is tender and delicious cooked just to this point.

Now drain the rice noodles and dry them well on paper towels. Pour oil into a heavy frying pan to a depth of 3.5-cm

(1½-inches), and heat it to 185°C (360°F). Toss in a third of the noodles and fry for 1 minute. Skim them out, place them on paper towels, and fry the remaining noodles in two batches. Make a bed of crisply browned noodles on a heated platter.

In another frying pan, heat 3 tablespoons oil. Toss in the mange-touts, spring onions, bean sprouts, celery, and mushrooms. Stir-fry over high heat for 2 to 3 minutes. Add the Worcestershire sauce, another teaspoon of pepper, and the reduced duck stock, and toss until everything is blended. Spoon the vegetables over the fried noodles and arrange the sliced duck breasts and legs around the outside of the platter.

PEKING CURRY–TOMATO SAUCE ON NOODLES

This was a regular offering in Chinese restaurants when I was a boy in Oregon. I never see it on restaurant menus any more, which is a shame: it has a strong tomato taste lightly flavoured with curry. Use it on dried or fresh Chinese noodles or with the Japanese Udon Noodles on page 51. Cellophane noodles are too delicate to stand up to the sauce.

6 TO 8 SERVINGS
225-g (8-oz) butter
2 onions, peeled and chopped
2 cloves garlic, finely chopped
1 tablespoon curry powder, or more to taste
Two 800-g (28-oz) tins Italian plum tomatoes
450-g (1-lb) minced beef
Salt
450-g (1-lb) Chinese or Japanese
*   whole-wheat noodles*

Melt the butter in a 2.5-litre (4½-pt) saucepan. Add the onions and garlic and cook them, stirring, until they are soft but not brown. Add the curry powder and cook for a minute to develop the flavour. Then add the tinned tomatoes and break them up with a wooden spoon. Reduce the heat, cover loosely, and simmer the sauce until it is thick, about 1½ hours. Break up the minced meat, drop it into the simmering sauce, and cook very gently, stirring often, for another half hour. Add salt to taste.

Cook the noodles. Drain them, and serve with the sauce.

PASTITSIO FOR A PARTY

This is one of the best Greek dishes I know, a good oven dish that's very rich and full flavoured. It comes from Leon Lianides, the owner of the Coach House in New York. Patrons of the Coach House know that you can't get Greek dishes there; for that, you have to visit Leon at his home.

12 SERVINGS
150-g (5-oz) onion, finely chopped
270-g (9½-oz) butter
2 cloves garlic, finely chopped
675-g (1½-lb) lean beef, minced
900-g (2-lb) lean lamb, minced
Salt and freshly ground black pepper
675-g (1½-lb) tomato sauce (p. 71)
1 teaspoon dried oregano
½ teaspoon cinnamon
½ teaspoon dried basil
1 bay leaf
40-g (1½-oz) finely chopped parsley
225-ml (8-fl oz) dry red wine

1.5 litres (2¾-pt) single cream
450-ml (16-fl oz) milk
175-g (6-oz) flour
Good pinch of nutmeg
10 egg yolks
450-g (1-lb) fresh Ricotta cheese
675-g (1½-lb) elbow macaroni or ziti
175-g (6-oz) grated Pecorino Romano cheese

First make your meat sauce. In a large frying pan cook the onion in 40-g (1½-oz) of the butter. When the onion is transparent, add the garlic and cook for 2 minutes. Add the meats and cook over high heat, breaking it up with a wooden spoon until the meat is no longer red. Season with ½ teaspoon salt, ½ teaspoon pepper, and the tomato sauce, oregano, cinnamon, basil, bay leaf, parsley, and wine. Cook the sauce, stirring frequently, until most of the liquid has been absorbed. This meat sauce can be prepared in advance and kept in the refrigerator or freezer until you are ready to use it. I never think that far ahead about what I plan to eat, but it's a useful idea if you are making the pastitsio for a party.

To make the cream sauce, bring all but 225-ml (8-fl oz) of the cream just to boiling point with the milk. In another saucepan, melt remaining butter. Add the flour, stirring with a wire whisk. When the roux is blended and smooth, pour in the hot cream and milk, stirring furiously with the whisk to keep it from going lumpy. Cook until the sauce is thick and smooth, about 15 minutes. Season with salt, pepper, and nutmeg. Turn off the heat and let the sauce cool for 10 minutes before you add the egg yolks.

In a bowl, beat the egg yolks with the remaining unheated cream. Gradually add about 425-ml (¾-pt) of the warm cream sauce to this egg mixture, beating all the while to make sure that the eggs don't curdle. Then pour the egg mixture into the cream sauce, continuing to stir until everything is blended. Finally, beat in the Ricotta.

Butter the inside of a large, deep baking dish. This recipe will need a dish at least 37.5 x 22.5 x 10-cm (15 x 9 x 4-inches). Cook and drain the macaroni. Place half the macaroni in the dish and sprinkle with half the cheese. Spoon on half the cream sauce, smoothing it with the back of a large spoon. Spread on all of the meat sauce. Now add the rest of the macaroni, the rest of the cream sauce, and the rest of the grated cheese, and place in a 200°C (400°F), Gas 6 oven. Bake for 55 minutes, when the pastitsio should be covered with a golden-brown crust.

If you want to serve it in neatly cut squares, you should finish cooking the pastitsio at least 6 hours before you intend to serve it. Leave it out on the kitchen counter or, if the day is warm, place it in the refrigerator. Then cut the casserole into serving portions and reheat before serving.

LEON LIANIDES'S LEG OF LAMB WITH ORZO

Orzo is a kind of pasta that is rice-like in shape and, almost, in taste. It's an especial favourite with the Greeks and lends itself agreeably to hot dishes, soups, and salads. Use it instead of rice or potatoes as a side dish, with just some butter and a good sprinkle of cheese. You'll find that it won't become gummy as rice may. In this preparation, the orzo soaks up all the wonderfully meaty juices that come from the lamb.

8 SERVINGS
2.3–3.6-kg (5—8-lb) leg of lamb
Juice of 1 lemon
2 cloves garlic, halved
Pinch of dried oregano

½ teaspoon dried basil
½ teaspoon dried mint
Salt and freshly ground black pepper
2 onions, coarsely chopped
1.4-kg (3-lb, 3-oz) tinned Italian plum tomatoes
1.5 litres (2¾-pt) good beef or chicken stock
350-g (12-oz) orzo
Grated hard cheese

Preheat the oven to 230°C (450°C), Gas 8. Rub the meat with the lemon juice, split garlic cloves, oregano, basil, mint, salt, and pepper. Place it on a rack in a large roasting pan, with the chopped onions underneath. Place in the oven, and after 20 minutes, turn the heat down to 180°C (350°F), Gas 4. Add the tomatoes and about 425-ml (¾-pt) stock to the onions under the pan. Cook the lamb for another 60 minutes, until the outside of the meat is golden brown and the internal temperature registers 135°C (275°F). The inside will be medium rare, but after it has been kept warm on a heated platter while you cook the orzo, it will be pink and juicy.

Take the lamb off its rack and put it on a heated platter. Scrape all the solids from the bottom of the roasting pan, and pour the juices through a strainer. Return the liquid to the pan with the remaining meat or chicken stock. Bring to the boil on top of the stove and gradually add the orzo. Stir well, and return the pan to the oven. Cook, stirring now and then, until the orzo is cooked and the liquid is all absorbed. When it's nearly done, carve the meat.

Take the orzo from the oven, turn it into a bowl or onto a serving platter, and sprinkle it with grated cheese. I've also had orzo cooked this way with cubes of fetta cheese mixed through it. Serve some of the orzo alongside the sliced lamb on each plate.

BEEF AND SCALLOPS WITH CELLOPHANE NOODLES

This recipe is derived from one that I taught during a series of classes on 'Taste' with Barbara Kafka. The beef and scallops make an interesting combination, and are delicate enough in flavour to work with cellophane noodles.

6 SERVINGS
450-g (1-lb) cellophane noodles
2 tablespoons oil
450-g (1-lb) beef fillet, in strips
  5 x 1-cm (2 x ½-inch)
350-g (¾-lb) small shelled scallops, or about
  8 larger scallops, thickly sliced
1 large clove garlic, crushed
175-g (6-oz) spring onions, sliced diagonally
1 teaspoon salt
Freshly ground black pepper
¼ teaspoon dried red chili-pepper flakes

Prepare the cellophane noodles early in the day. Do not soak them. Just break them apart and deep-fry in oil heated to 190°C (375°F) for a few seconds until they puff up. Drain on paper towels.

Heat the oil in a frying pan. Add the beef, scallops, and garlic all at once and cook over high heat, stirring, for about 2 minutes. Add the spring onions, salt, pepper, and dried chili-pepper. Cook for another 30 seconds, stirring furiously, and pour over a platter holding the fried cellophane noodles.

BEACH PÂTÉ

This is a meat loaf that has tiny pasta shells scattered through it. The shells make a pattern like the bits of tongue or pistachio nuts that are found in pâté de campagne. They're fun, but if you can't find them, try orzo, tubetti, funghini — any small, granular-shaped pasta. I've made this for years and years. It's a perfect dish to take on a picnic and slice on the spot. Hence the name.

8 SERVINGS
100-g (4-oz) very small pasta
about 150-g (5-oz) carrots, cut in 2.5-cm
  (1-inch) sections
2 medium onions
4 large cloves garlic
25-g (1-oz) chopped parsley
2 teaspoons dried thyme
1 teaspoon freshly ground black pepper
2 teaspoons salt
900-g (2-lb) good lean stewing steak,
  minced twice
450-g (1-lb) pork shoulder, minced twice
50-g (2-oz) fresh breadcrumbs
2 eggs, lightly beaten
6 rashers streaky bacon

Cook and drain the pasta. Put the carrots, onions, garlic, parsley, thyme, pepper, and salt in the food processor and process for 30 seconds until they are well mixed. Turn this mixture into a large bowl and add the beef, pork, breadcrumbs, eggs, and the pasta shells. I like to use my hands for this job, but if you are squeamish, use wooden spoons. Form the meat mixture into a firm oval loaf.

Make a bed in a shallow baking pan with 3 bacon rashers. Place the meat loaf on the bed of bacon, and put the remaining strips across the top. Bake in a 180°C (350°F), Gas 4 oven for 1½ hours, and serve hot or cold. You will find that if you make your meat loaf free-form instead of in a loaf tin, you'll get a firmer texture for slicing and plenty of flavourful outer crust.

121

CHILI SHORT RIBS AND MACARONI

I've always been a devotee of beef ribs, no matter how they are done: boiled, braised, or barbecued. I like the combination in this treatment of sweetcorn, macaroni, and chili. It should be hot, but not five-alarm hot. If you can find corn or maize macaroni, it makes a good addition to the dish. The term 'short rib' describes the thin ribs of beef remaining when the foreribs are removed.

6 SERVINGS
2.3-kg (5-lb) lean short ribs, cut in pieces
3 large onions, thinly sliced
6 gloves garlic, crushed
4 tablespoons mild chili powder
1 teaspoon cumin
1 tablespoon salt
1 small chili pepper
450-g (1-lb) home-made tomato sauce
350—450-ml (12—16-fl oz) beef stock
1½ teaspoons hot chili powder, or to taste
about 225-g (8-oz) fresh or frozen
    sweetcorn kernels
450-g (1-lb) short-cut macaroni
    (preferably corn)
50-g (2-oz) butter
25-g (1-oz) chopped parsley
50-g (2-oz) grated mild Cheddar cheese

Place the short ribs on their sides in a grill pan from which the rack has been removed. Grill 15-cm (6-inches) from the heat until the meat is brown. Turn the ribs, and grill until the other side is brown and crisp.

In a casserole, mix the onions, garlic, mild chili powder, cumin, salt, chili pepper, and tomato sauce. Lay the ribs over the mixture, and pour on enough beef stock to cover. Cover the casserole and place in a 180°C (350°F), Gas 4 oven. After 45 minutes, check to see if more stock is needed. Stir in the hot chili powder and cook for another 45 minutes, or until the meat is tender. Then add the sweetcorn kernels.

(If you prepare the ribs and sauce ahead of time, you will be able to chill the casserole and remove the fat that hardens on the top, before you reheat it.)

Cook the macaroni and drain. Toss with the butter, chopped parsley, a few spoonfuls of sauce, and the cheese. Make a bed of the pasta on a serving platter. Arrange the ribs on it, and spoon the rest of the sauce over everything.

LASAGNE

Often baked pasta dishes are a bore, but this one holds up, I think, because all the different sauces are first-rate and the final cooking is brief. It looks like a long recipe, but once you have prepared the different elements, you can put it together in a matter of minutes.

6 TO 8 SERVINGS
1 recipe Light Tomato Sauce (p. 71)

MEATBALLS:
225-g (8-oz) chuck steak, minced
225-g (8-oz) sausagemeat
2 onions, finely chopped
1 small chili pepper, seeds removed
15-g (½-oz) chopped parsley
2 teaspoons Pesto (p. 70)
½ teaspoon salt
½ teaspoon freshly ground black pepper
Pinch nutmeg
1 egg

BÉCHAMEL SAUCE:

40-g (1½-oz) butter
4 tablespoons flour
450-ml (16-fl oz) good chicken stock
⅛ teaspoon nutmeg
1 teaspoon salt
½ teaspoon freshly ground black pepper
225-ml (8-fl oz) double cream
100-g (4-oz) white lasagne
100-g (4-oz) whole-wheat lasagne
2 tablespoons peanut or olive oil
25-g (1-oz) butter
100-g (4-oz) Gruyère cheese, grated
100-g (4-oz) Parmesan cheese, grated

Make the tomato sauce and set aside.

To make the meatballs, put everything into a large bowl. Using your hands, blend the ingredients thoroughly and make small balls, about the size of large cherries. Refrigerate until needed.

To make the béchamel sauce, melt the butter in a heavy saucepan. Stir in the flour, and cook for 2 to 3 minutes, until the mixture is smooth and golden. Remove from the heat while you add the chicken broth, stirring vigorously. Return the pan to the heat and stir with a spatula or wire whisk until the sauce is smooth and thick. Simmer for 3 to 4 minutes. Season with the nutmeg, salt, and pepper. Add the cream, and keep the mixture just below the simmer for a few minutes to blend the flavours.

To assemble the lasagne, bring about 3.5 litres (6½-pt) water to the boil. Cook the lasagne strips, 3 or 4 at a time, until they are just done. Remove them with a slotted spoon, dip in cold water to stop the cooking, and lay on a dish towel. Continue until all the pasta is cooked.

Melt the 2 tablespoons of oil and the butter in a large heavy frying pan. When the fats have blended and are hot, but not smoking, add the meatballs. Cook over medium-high heat, shaking the pan constantly to keep the meatballs in motion, until lightly browned all over. Be sure to keep them hopping in the pan so they do not flatten.

Spoon a thin layer of tomato sauce onto the bottom of a 35-cm (14-inch) baking dish. Make a layer of white pasta over the sauce. Spread on more tomato sauce, and sprinkle with meatballs. Spoon on half the béchamel. Continue with a layer of whole-wheat pasta, tomato sauce, and meatballs and so forth until they are all used up, alternating white and whole-wheat lasagne and ending with the béchamel. Sprinkle with the grated cheeses and bake in a 230°C (450°F), Gas 8 oven for 15 minutes.

SAVOURY TONGUE WITH FINE NOODLES

I love the delicate flavour of calf tongue. When I can get them, I will often simmer small tongues in seasoned stock, then let them cool and slice them thin to use in sandwiches, in salads, or in this assertive topping for pasta.

4 TO 6 SERVINGS
1 recipe Light Tomato Sauce (p. 71)
65—75-g (2½—3-oz) chopped onion
1 teaspoon salt
Freshly ground black pepper
¼ teaspoon Tabasco
450-g (1-lb) finely chopped cooked calf's or ox tongue (lamb's could be used too)
450-g (1-lb) spaghettini or angel's hair pasta
Grated Parmesan cheese

Combine the tomato sauce with the chopped onion, seasonings, and tongue in a 1.7-litre (3-pt) saucepan. Cook gently for 10 minutes.

Cook and drain the pasta. Then spoon the sauce over the cooked noodles and sprinkle with a *great* deal of Parmesan cheese.

OSSI BUCHI WITH ORZO

I've always objected to getting big chunks of ossi buchi on my plate. If you can get your butcher to cut the long bones in pieces only 2.5-cm (1-inch) thick, you will find that they are still meaty and beautiful, and will cook very quickly.

4 TO 6 SERVINGS

about 1.8-kg (4-lb) hind knuckle of veal,
   cut in 2.5-cm (1-inch) pieces
100-ml (4-fl oz) olive oil
2 teaspoons salt
2 teaspoons freshly ground black pepper
at least 850-ml (1½-pt) chicken stock
2 teaspoons dried basil
175-g (6-oz) orzo
25-g (1-oz) butter
1 teaspoon powdered saffron

GREMOLATA:
4 large cloves garlic, chopped
40-g (1½-oz) chopped parsley
Zest of 2 lemons

Sear the veal in the oil in a large pan over moderate heat, turning each piece once or twice. Season with salt and pepper and pour in about 225-ml (8-fl oz) chicken stock. Cover the pan and simmer the meat for 20 minutes. Remove the lid, add the basil, and simmer for another 20 to 25 minutes.

Meanwhile, cook the orzo in the remaining chicken stock. When it is done, drain, reserving about 50-ml (2-fl oz) stock in which to soak the saffron for a few minutes.

Toss the orzo with the butter and saffron and its liquid.

To make the gremolata, chop the garlic and parsley together with a chef's knife and grate the lemon into the mixture.

Serve the ossi buchi on a bed of orzo, and sprinkle gremolata over the top.

SAUSAGE–TOMATO SAUCE OVER PENNE

This is a hearty sauce and deserves a substantial pasta, something like penne, the little pointed quills, or ziti, or one of the twists. The seasoning depends on the seasoning of your sausages.

4 TO 6 SERVINGS
1 recipe Light Tomato Sauce (p. 71),
  without the butter
225-g (8-oz) fresh Italian sausages
450-g (1-lb) pasta

Make the sauce. While it is cooking, cut the sausages into thin slices. Cook them for about 5 minutes in a heavy frying pan until the fat has drained out and the meat is cooked through. Pour off most of the fat, and add the meat to the sauce, with a little fat. Simmer together for 5 minutes while you cook and drain the pasta. Serve sauce over pasta.

PORK WITH SAUERKRAUT NOODLES

An admirable way to use leftover pork loin. If you don't have leftover pork, you can start fresh with thin slices of pork tenderloin, boned pork chops, shoulder, or leg. And, if you use smoked pork, you'll get something else — but something very nice!

6 SERVINGS
25-g (1-oz) butter
1 tablespoon oil
300—350-g (10—12-oz) cooked pork, or
   675—900-g (1½—2-lb) fresh pork, thinly sliced
2 tablespoons hot Hungarian paprika
350-ml (12-fl oz) white wine
350-g (12-oz) sauerkraut, rinsed and drained
1 teaspoon caraway seeds
450-g (1-lb) Continental egg noodles
Salt and freshly ground black pepper
100-ml (4-fl oz) double cream

Heat the butter with the oil in a heavy frying pan. Brown the pork slices on each side over fairly high heat, about 3 minutes to a side. Remove the meat, add the paprika, and cook in the fat for 1 minute. Pour in the wine and bring to a boil, stirring up the flavourful bits on the bottom of the pan. Cook until the wine is reduced slightly, then return the meat to the pan with the drained sauerkraut and caraway seeds. Simmer 10 to 12 minutes.

Cook and drain the noodles. Stir them into the pork-and-sauerkraut mixture and turn gently over medium heat, adding the cream as you do so.

SOFT NOODLES SAUTÉED

Because I live so near New York's Chinatown, I can buy fresh Chinese noodles when I make this lo mein. You can do nearly as well with dried Chinese noodles. If you can't find those, thin spaghetti makes an adequate substitute. The trick with this dish, as in most Chinese cooking, is to cook everything very rapidly. You get all the ingredients prepared ahead of time so that the actual cooking takes no more than 5 minutes.

4 SERVINGS

225-g (8-oz) Chinese noodles
225-g (8-oz) roast pork
1 bunch spring onions
2 ten-pence sized slices fresh ginger
2 cloves garlic
450-g (1-lb) bean sprouts
2½ tablespoons soy sauce
2½ tablespoons oyster sauce (available in
    Chinese grocers)
½ teaspoon salt
3 tablespoons peanut oil
1 tablespoon dry sherry
25-g (1-oz) chopped fresh coriander leaves

Cook and drain the noodles. Slice the meat into matchsticks. Cut the spring onions into 5-cm (2-inch) pieces and then into lengthwise shreds. Peel the ginger and cut the slices into matchsticks. Peel and mince the garlic. Rinse the bean sprouts in cold water. Pick them over, drain them, and set them aside. Combine the soy sauce, oyster sauce, and salt in a tea-cup and set aside.

Heat a wok or a large frying pan until it is very hot. Pour in the oil. Add the ginger and garlic, the pork shreds and spring onions, and stir-fry briskly for a minute. Pour in the sherry, continuing to mix rapidly. Add the bean sprouts while you toss furiously. Pour in the soy-sauce mixture as you stir.

Now add the noodles. Scoop them with the vegetables and meat, running your spatula underneath them, turning them over in the air, and letting them fall back into the fat. Stir-fry over high heat for 3 minutes, until everything is hot and coloured with the soy sauce. Sprinkle with the coriander, give one more stir, and pour into a hot serving dish.

VARIATIONS
- Instead of the pork, you could substitute slivers of

chicken breast, roast beef, or tiny shrimps. Instead of some of the bean sprouts you could use thinly sliced Chinese leaves, mange-touts, or bamboo shoots.

TAGLIARINI VERDI AL GUANCIALE

Where I live, in Greenwich Village, there is no end to wonderful Italian shops, and I have no trouble buying pancetta, the Italian unsmoked belly of pork. If you can't locate pancetta, you can substitute prosciutto, unsmoked ham, or bacon that has been simmered in water for 10 minutes, drained, and rinsed with fresh cold water.

6 SERVINGS
8 to 10 medium leeks
75-g (3-oz) butter
½ teaspoon freshly ground black pepper
2 tablespoons chopped flat-leaved parsley
Pinch of nutmeg
Salt
225-g (8-oz) sliced pancetta, ham or bacon,
   rinsed and cut into 1-cm (½-inch) pieces
550-g (1¼-lb) green tagliarini or other pasta
225-ml (8-fl oz) double cream
40-g (1½-oz) grated Parmesan cheese

Trim off the root ends and most of the green parts of the leeks. Slit the tops and wash thoroughly under running water to remove the grit. Cut into julienne strips and pat dry with paper towels.

Melt 25-g (1-oz) of the butter in a frying pan. Add the leeks, pepper, parsley, nutmeg, and salt. Sauté briskly until the leeks are golden, and remove them from the pan with a slotted spoon. Turn up the heat and sauté the pancetta until it is nearly crisp. Return the leeks to the pan and turn off the heat.

Melt the remaining butter in a large saucepan. Cook and drain the pasta and add to the pan. Stir as you add the leeks and pancetta. Blend in the cream and half the cheese, and cook gently for 2 minutes more over very low heat. Serve with the rest of the cheese and freshly ground black pepper on the side.

GNOCCHI À LA PARISIENNE

Years ago this was a regular feature on the luncheon menu at the Restaurant Madeleine in Paris. With a green salad, a dry white wine or champagne, and the raspberries to follow, it was sheer luxury. But, if you look closely at the recipe, you'll recognise plain old dumplings, made, this time, with a choux pastry.

4 SERVINGS
CHOUX PASTRY:
100-ml (4-fl oz) milk
100-ml (4-fl oz) water
¼ teaspoon salt
100-g (4-oz) butter
100-g (4-oz) flour
5 eggs

Four 10-cm (4-inch) vol-au-vents,
  or one 20-cm (9-inch) vol-au-vent
100-g (4-oz) butter
125—175-g (4—6-oz) sliced mushrooms
3 tablespoons flour
450-ml (16-fl oz) milk, warmed
5 tablespoons Madeira
450-g (1-lb) diced smoked ham
½ teaspoon salt
¼ teaspoon nutmeg
Grated cheese

131

First make the choux pastry. Put the milk, water, salt, and butter in a saucepan. Bring mixture to a boil over high heat. As soon as it boils, remove the pan from the heat and begin to add the flour. Beat the mixture with a wooden spoon while you slowly pour the flour into the pan. When all the flour has been added, set the pan back over the heat and beat vigorously for another minute. As part of the water evaporates, the pastry will become smooth and pull away from the sides of the pan. Remove the pan from the heat and set it aside to cool for 5 minutes. Make a well in the centre of the pastry, and beat in the eggs, 1 at a time, beating thoroughly after each addition.

When the eggs are absorbed and the mixture is smooth and glossy, spoon it into a piping bag that is fitted with a plain 2-cm (¾-inch) tube. Have a large pot of salted water at the boil. Twist the pastry bag tightly, forcing the dough to the bottom. Squeeze it out into the water, cutting it off in 2-cm (¾-inch) pieces. If you don't have a piping bag, you can just take up spoonfuls of dough and push them into the boiling water with a second spoon. Let the gnocchi cook in the boiling water for 2 or 3 minutes. When they rise to the top, skim them off with a slotted spoon and plunge immediately into a bowl of cold water to stop the cooking. Drain and dry on a paper towel.

Put the vol-au-vents to warm in a slow oven while you make the filling. Melt 50-g (2-oz) butter in a saucepan. Add the mushrooms and sauté them quickly. Add the remaining butter and the flour and stir them over moderate heat for about 3 minutes. Add the milk and Madeira gradually, stirring all the time, and cook for 5 minutes. Stir in the diced ham and gnocchi and season with salt and nutmeg.

Fill the warmed vol-au-vents with the gnocchi-mushroom-ham mixture. Sprinkle with cheese.

EGGS AND CHEESE

CHÈVRE-TOMATO SPAGHETTI
(with blue cheese)

PASTA CON QUATRO FORMAGGI

SPAGHETTI CARBONARA
(with prosciutto · with pork sausage ·
noodle patties)

PASTA AND CHEESE ROLL IN TOMATO SAUCE

MACARONI AND CHEESE

BASIL LASAGNE

WHOLE-WHEAT-NOODLE CASSEROLE

MACARONI WITH MUSTARD-CHEESE

ORZO SOUFFLÉ

ANGEL'S-HAIR SOUFFLÉ

CHÈVRE–TOMATO SPAGHETTI

This combination of tomato and goat cheese is just delicious. Chèvre softens in an especially creamy way; it seems to relax into the sauce. Make the sauce in a pan that's large enough so that you can pour the drained spaghetti into it and let it cook for about 2 minutes, long enough to soak up some of the flavour.

> 4 TO 6 SERVINGS
> 1 recipe Light Tomato Sauce (p. 71)
> 100-g (4-oz) chèvre, cut in chunks
> ¼ to ½ teaspoon Tabasco, or to taste
> 450-g (1-lb) spaghetti

When the sauce is finished, add the chunks of cheese to it and let them soften. Season to taste with Tabasco: it should be quite spicy.

Cook and drain the spaghetti. Then add the drained spaghetti to the pan and let it cook for a few minutes more.

VARIATION
● Instead of chèvre, use a little less blue cheese and eliminate the Tabasco.

PASTA CON QUATRO FORMAGGI

The only requirement for the four cheeses in this dish is that one of them be Parmesan. Evan Jones, in his *World of Cheese*, makes it with Bel Paese, Fontina, Gorgonzola, and Parmesan. It's not traditional, but I like to use a goat cheese in this dish. It doesn't quite melt; it softens and becomes thick. But by all means go ahead and experiment: this is an excellent opportunity to use up all the leftover cheese in the refrigerator.

4 TO 6 SERVINGS
100-g (4-oz) butter
450-g (1-lb) penne or ziti
50-g (2-oz) goat cheese, in chunks
40-g (1½-oz) grated Parmesan cheese
50-g (2-oz) grated Pecorino Romano cheese
50-g (2-oz) shredded Gruyère cheese
Freshly ground black pepper

Melt the butter in a heavy saucepan. Cook and drain the pasta and add to the melted butter. Then mix in the cheeses, one at a time, turning the noodles thoroughly as you go. Serve very hot with lots of freshly ground black pepper.

SPAGHETTI CARBONARA

The trick is not to wind up with scrambled eggs, and that can be managed only if you add the egg mixture to the hot noodles very slowly, tossing them like a demon all the while. Some books specify bacon in a carbonara, and others pancetta. It's not traditional, but I like to use real Smithfield ham, because it tastes better and it never becomes fatty and flabby as bacon does.

4 TO 6 SERVINGS
4 eggs
2 tablespoons double cream
Salt and freshly ground black pepper
225-g (8-oz) baked ham, cut in slivers
450-g (1-lb) spaghetti
100-g (4-oz) mixed grated Parmesan and
    Caciocavallo cheeses

In a small bowl, beat the eggs with the cream, salt, pepper, and ham.

Cook the spaghetti, and when it is drained return it to the pan over a turned-off burner. Give the egg mixture another stir and then begin to mix it gently and slowly into the spaghetti, keeping it moving all the while so that the eggs don't cook. Add the cheese and continue to toss the noodles until everything is blended. Serve immediately with more grated cheese.

VARIATIONS
* Instead of the Smithfield ham (made from peanut-fed hogs from Virginia), use another good cured ham, use 225-g (8-oz) prosciutto cut in slivers, or 225-g (8-oz) good, tasty, cooked pork sausages out of their skins.
* (One of the pleasant aftermaths of Spaghetti Carbonara is a plate of sautéed pasta patties. I can't give proper measurements for this dish because you just use whatever you have left over, but you'll wind up with patties that are crisp and brown on the outside, chewy on the inside, and just delicious with roast pork or grilled chicken.

To make the pasta patties, melt 100-g (4-oz) butter in a heavy frying pan. Then pull off clumps of the cold leftover spaghetti in patty-sized pieces. When the butter is nice and hot, place 3 or 4 patties in it. Let them brown on both sides; the eggs and cheese will hold them together as they cook. Take them out of the pan and drain them on paper towels while you make the rest of the patties.)

PASTA AND CHEESE ROLL IN TOMATO SAUCE

This is an amusing variation on a Swiss roll. I love the tiny acini di pepe, which look like peppercorns, but you could use any other really small pasta. Try any pastina — orzo, for instance, or star-shaped stellini. They have to be light enough so that they don't drag down the soufflé mixture.

4 TO 6 SERVINGS
150—175-g (5—6-oz) tiny pasta
6 eggs, separated
50-g (2-oz) butter, melted
1 teaspoon dried oregano
¼ teaspoon thyme
Salt and freshly ground black pepper
6 tablespoons grated Parmesan cheese
175-g (6-oz) shredded Mozzarella cheese
350-ml (12-fl oz) Light Tomato Sauce (p. 71)

Butter a 37.5 x 27.5-cm (15 x 11-inch) Swiss roll tin. Line it with greaseproof paper or aluminium foil, leaving an overhang of about 5-cm (2-inches) at each end. Butter the paper well to prevent the eggs from sticking.

Cook and drain the pasta.

Beat the egg yolks until they are light and lemon-coloured, then gradually stir in the pasta, butter, oregano, thyme, salt, pepper, and 2 tablespoons of the Parmesan cheese. In another bowl, beat the egg whites until they hold soft, unwavering peaks. Fold the whites into the yolk mixture quite thoroughly. Spread the mixture into the prepared tin, smoothing it with a knife or a rubber spatula so that it is the same thickness overall. Sprinkle it evenly with Mozzarella and bake it in a 190°C (375°F), Gas 5 oven for 15 minutes, until it is firm and puffy. Take it out of the oven and turn the oven temperature down to 160°C (325°F), Gas 3.

With most roulade mixtures, you would now quickly invert the pan onto a towel and peel off the paper. But you want to keep the Mozzarella on the inside of the roll; so, instead, you grasp the extended ends of the grease-proof paper or foil, lift it out of the pan, and lay it on a large cooling rack. Let it cool for 10 minutes, and then use the paper to help roll it up, starting with one long side. As you roll, peel off the paper. You may have to use a small, sharp knife to help you along.

Slice the roll into 10 rounds. Arrange them in an overlapping row in a buttered baking dish. Cover them with tomato sauce, sprinkle with the remaining Parmesan, and heat at 160°C (325°F), Gas 3 for 20 minutes, until the cheese is melted.

MACARONI AND CHEESE

This is a great classic dish. It has to be gooey, made with a really rich béchamel and with a Cheddar that sings with flavour. I love it when the cheese on top gets burnt and chewy, and I love to scrape up the dried bits that stick to the pan.

4 TO 6 SERVINGS
50-g (2-oz) butter
4 tablespoons flour
450-ml (16-fl oz) milk
Dash of freshly ground black pepper
½ teaspoon Tabasco, or more to taste
100-ml (4-fl oz) double cream
225-g (8-oz) short-cut macaroni
350-g (12-oz) grated Cheddar cheese

Melt the butter in a saucepan over low heat. Add the flour, and stir it with a wooden spoon or spatula for about 3 minutes, until the roux is frothy and the taste of raw flour is gone. Meanwhile, heat the milk in another pan. Add the warm milk gradually to the roux, stirring hard all the while. Turn up the heat and cook, stirring, until the sauce is just at the boiling point. Turn down the heat and let it simmer for a few minutes. Now add the pepper and Tabasco. Don't be afraid of the Tabasco: it will help to bring out the taste of the cheese. Stir in the double cream and simmer a little longer, until the flavours are blended.

Cook and drain the macaroni.

Mix three-quarters of the grated cheese into the simmering sauce. As soon as it melts, combine it with the drained macaroni, and pour it into a baking pan. Sprinkle the top with the remaining cheese, and bake for 20 to 30 minutes in a 180°C (350°F), Gas 4 oven.

BASIL LASAGNE

A thin and elegant version of lasagne, just two layers of pasta with basil-flavoured Ricotta in between. Serve it at lunch, with a cool white wine and a green salad.

3 OR 4 SERVINGS
225-g (8-oz) lasagne
75-g (3-oz) Pesto (p. 71)
225-g (8-oz) Ricotta cheese
1 egg
40-g (1½-oz) grated Parmesan cheese
225-g (8-oz) Mozzarella cheese, shredded

Put the lasagne into a large pan of boiling water.

Meanwhile, using a wooden spoon or the food processor, beat the pesto, Ricotta, egg, and Parmesan cheese until they are well blended. Butter a shallow baking dish. Drain the lasagne when just done al dente and make a layer of it in the baking dish. Cover it with the Ricotta-pesto mixture and then with a second layer of lasagne. Over this, spread all the Mozzarella and sprinkle with more Parmesan cheese. Bake in a 180°C (350°F), Gas 4 oven for 25 minutes.

WHOLE-WHEAT–NOODLE CASSEROLE

I love the texture of whole-wheat noodles. They seem to have so much character. This is a good oven dish, a different way to have a starch dish with steak, sausages, or fried chicken.

6 SERVINGS
450-g (1-lb) whole-wheat noodles
350-g (12-oz) cottage cheese
225-ml (8-fl oz) yogurt
1 tablespoon Dijon mustard
1 teaspoon freshly ground black pepper
1 tablespoon Worcestershire sauce
100-g (4-oz) Gruyère or Cheddar
cheese, shredded

Cook and drain the noodles.

Combine the noodles, cottage cheese, yogurt, mustard, pepper, and Worcestershire sauce. Turn into a buttered baking dish and sprinkle the shredded cheese over the top. Bake in a 180°C (350°F), Gas 4 oven for 30 minutes.

MACARONI WITH MUSTARD–CHEESE

This is a natural to serve at a barbecue with hamburgers or hot dogs. The mustard adds a wonderful tang, and if you're watching your weight, you can simply use low-fat cottage cheese.

6 TO 8 SERVINGS
450-g (1-lb) macaroni
450-g (1-lb) cottage cheese
2 tablespoons Dijon mustard
1 teaspoon freshly ground black pepper

Cook and drain the macaroni.

Combine it with the other ingredients and toss well. Although part of the appeal is in the contrast between the hot noodles and cold cheese, this dish can also be mixed ahead of time and served cold or, rather, at room temperature.

ORZO SOUFFLÉ

The secret of this soufflé is the egg! The yolks and their
treatment are all-important. It is made without the usual
béchamel base, so that you have to beat the egg whites until
they form soft peaks, and then fold them into the rest of
the mixture so that they stay full of air. Then relax and
let your souffle do its thing. Serve as soon as it comes out
of the oven, making sure that everybody gets a big piece
of the browned crust as well as some of the creamy centre.

> 4 SERVINGS
> 6 egg yolks
> about 350-g (12-oz) cooked orzo, drained
> 75-g (3-oz) grated Parmesan cheese, or grated
>   Gruyère cheese, or 50-g (2-oz) grated Cheddar cheese
> ¼ teaspoon salt
> ½ teaspoon freshly ground black pepper
> Several dashes Tabasco
> 8 egg whites

Put the egg yolks in the bowl of a mixer and beat them
until they are thick and lemon-coloured, as long as 5 minutes.
Beating the eggs very well allows you to make the soufflé
without a flour thickening. Add the orzo, the grated cheese,
salt, pepper, and Tabasco.

In another bowl, preferably copper, beat the egg whites
with a wire whisk or an electric mixer. Beat until they are
stiff but not dry. Do not overbeat until they stand upright
as though you were making meringues. Stir a large spoonful
of white into the yolk mixture. Then fold in the rest of the
whites, cutting lightly through the centre of the mixture
with the side of the spatula, pulling it up and over and then
cutting down again.

Pour into a buttered 1.7-litre (3-pt) soufflé dish and
smooth the top with the spatula. Draw a circle with your
finger on top of the mixture about 5-cm (2-inches) in from
the rim. This will make the soufflé form a cap that rises

143

higher than the rim. Bake in a preheated 190°C (375°F), Gas 5 oven for about 25 minutes, and serve immediately.

ANGEL'S–HAIR SOUFFLÉ

When the soufflé rises, it lifts the very thin strands of pasta and bits of prosciutto with it. Use your imagination when you pick the cheese. I've suggested Cheddar, Gruyère, or Parmesan, all of which have good character and melting qualities. But you might want to try a fresh Mozzarella or delicate Fontina instead.

4 SERVINGS
125-g (4-oz) angel's-hair pasta
6 egg yolks
100-g (3½-oz) shredded Cheddar, Parmesan,
*   or Gruyère cheese*
175-g (6-oz) finely diced prosciutto
½ teaspoon freshly ground black pepper
⅛ teaspoon Tabasco
8 egg whites

Cook and drain the pasta.

Put the egg yolks in the bowl of your mixer and beat them until they are thick and butter-coloured, as long as 5 minutes. Stir in the cheese, prosciutto, pepper, Tabasco, and the cooked pasta.

In another bowl, beat the egg whites until they form soft peaks that just bend over. Stir a large spoonful of the white into the yolk mixture, and then fold in the rest of the beaten whites gently but thoroughly, using a rubber spatula.

Pour the mixture into a buttered 1.7-litre (3-pt) soufflé dish and smooth the top with the spatula. Draw a circle with your finger on top of the soufflé about 5·cm (2-inches) in from the rim. This will make the centre rise higher than the sides to form a cap. Bake in the centre of a preheated 190°C (375°F), Gas 5 oven for 15 to 20 minutes.

STUFFED PASTAS

STUFFED SHELLS
(with Italian sausage ·
vinaigrette · other stuffings)

SPINACH RAVIOLI

RAVIOLI WITH SWEETBREAD STUFFING

CRABMEAT RAVIOLI
(with tuna · shrimps or
prawns · scallops)

STUFFED ZITI

KREPLACH

WONTONS

TORTELLINI

FROGS' LEGS TORTELLONI

STEAMED MEAT PACKETS

NOODLE-AUBERGINE DUMPLINGS

STUFFED SHELLS

This is one of those clean-out-the-refrigerator recipes. It is absolutely delicious when made with cooked chicken. But it can be made as well with leftover beef, ham, or veal, and is a wonderful solution for the very last scraps of the Christmas turkey.

6 TO 8 SERVINGS
Meat from 2 chicken legs and thighs, or
  350—450-g (12—16-oz) any leftover meat
225-g (8-oz) mushrooms
3 large cloves garlic
6 sprigs parsley
2 teaspoons dried tarragon
1 egg
1 teaspoon salt
1 teaspoon freshly ground black pepper
½ teaspoon Tabasco
1 tablespoon lemon juice
Thirty 5-cm (2-inch) macaroni shells
  (conchiglie)
225-g (8-oz) grated Gruyère cheese
1 recipe Light Tomato Sauce (p. 71)

Combine the meat, mushrooms, garlic, parsley, tarragon, egg, salt, pepper, Tabasco, and lemon juice in the bowl of the food processor and process until mixture is well blended.

Cook and drain the shells, and spoon some of the filling into each of the cooked shells. Lay them in a buttered baking dish, open sides up. Sprinkle with most of the cheese, cover with tomato sauce, and then with the rest of the cheese. Bake in a preheated 180°C (350°F), Gas 4 oven for 30 minutes, until bubbling hot.

VARIATIONS
● Instead of leftover meat, you could use some spicy Italian sausage meat, and stuff the shells with it. The sausage

should be seasoned well enough so that it won't require any other seasoning. Cover it with the cheese and tomato sauce as suggested, although you may prefer to use an Italian cheese.

• Cold, previously cooked shells lend themselves to several combinations. Drain and dry on a rack after cooking. Stuff and arrange on a bed of greens. Spread a pungent vinaigrette over the stuffed shells and garnish with chopped chives and parsley.

• Suggested Stuffings for Shells
    1. Well-seasoned shrimp or prawn salad
    2. Crab or lobster salad
    3. A brightly flavoured chicken salad

• Your salad plate may be garnished with onion rings and black olives, cherry tomatoes, and hard-boiled eggs.

SPINACH RAVIOLI

Making ravioli is one of those skills that is perfectly simple — once you know how. Don't be put off if your first tries are messy. You might want to practise on this spinach-and-ricotta-stuffed ravioli and then, once you've got the knack, go on to a more expensive filling.

4 TO 6 SERVINGS
1 recipe French Noodles (p. 49)

STUFFING:
1.1-kg (2½-lb) fresh spinach, or two
    300-g (10-oz) packets frozen spinach
1 large clove garlic
½ teaspoon nutmeg
100-g (4-oz) Ricotta cheese
½ teaspoon Tabasco
1 teaspoon salt

149

SAUCE:
100-g (4-oz) butter, melted
100-g (4-oz) Gruyère cheese, grated
25-g (1-oz) chopped parsley

Prepare the pasta dough and let it rest.

Plunge the spinach into boiling water, let wilt for 1 minute, and drain. Place it in a hand towel and squeeze out all the liquid. If you use frozen spinach, defrost it and squeeze it dry in the same manner. Combine the spinach with the garlic, nutmeg, Ricotta, Tabasco, and salt in the food processor, and process until you have a smooth paste.

Roll out the pasta dough into 2 rectangular sheets. Drop tiny bits of filling, about ½ teaspoon each, at regular intervals across one sheet of pasta. Lay the second sheet over it and, using your fingertip, press down between the mounds of filling, forming squares. Cut along the edges of the squares with a pastry cutter, and seal edges with tines of a fork.

Another method is to use a ravioli tray. Lay a sheet of dough on the tray. Then spoon bits of filling into the shallow hollows on the tray. Lay a second sheet of dough over the first, and roll over the tray with an ordinary rolling pin, forming the ravioli.

A third method is to use one of the rolling pins that is specially marked for ravioli. Roll out a large sheet of dough. Then roll over it with the marked pin. Place dabs of stuffing inside the squares on half the dough, and fold the second half of the sheet over it. Cut along the markings. And, if you want to, there is nothing to prevent you from simply taking two sheets of pasta, cutting free-form squares with a knife, putting on the filling, and then using the fork around the edge. However they look, they'll taste just the same.

To cook the ravioli, bring a big pan of water to the boil. Drop in the ravioli, a few at a time, and cook for about 3 minutes after they float to the surface. Remove with a slotted spoon and place on a warm platter. Spoon the melted butter over the ravioli and sprinkle with cheese and parsley.

RAVIOLI WITH SWEETBREAD STUFFING

I wanted to do things with ravioli that weren't traditionally Italian, to use surprising seasonings and stuffings, and I think that they worked out very well. These tiny packages would make an excellent beginning to any dinner, no matter how formal.

4 TO 6 SERVINGS
1 recipe French Noodles (p. 49)

STUFFING:
1 sweetbread (calf or lamb)
1 brain (calf or lamb), soaked in cold water
1 chicken breast, boned
½ teaspoon Tabasco
2 teaspoons salt
2 egg whites
1 tablespoon fresh tarragon, or ½
   teaspoon dried tarragon
3 shallots or button onions
Pinch of nutmeg

SAUCE:
100-g (4-oz) butter
6 shallots or button onions, minced
   or finely chopped
3 large sprigs tarragon, or 2 teaspoons
   dried tarragon
25-g (1-oz) chopped parsley

Prepare the pasta dough and let it rest.

For the stuffing, put all the ingredients into the bowl of the food processor and process well. Set the puréed mixture in a steamer and steam over boiling water for 10 to 15 minutes, stirring it now and then with a wooden spoon. Don't let it cook too long, or it will become hard. If you make the stuffing ahead of time, refrigerate it until you are ready to use it, and then put it back in the processor and blend for a few minutes to lighten it and smooth it out.

Make and cook the ravioli by one of the methods described in the preceding recipe.

To make the sauce, melt the butter with shallots and herbs in a saucepan over gentle heat. Spoon over the cooked ravioli.

CRABMEAT RAVIOLI

I have a passion for crabmeat in all its forms, and I think that this crabmeat ravioli is something quite special, very delicate and unlike any ravioli you've ever had.

4 TO 6 SERVINGS
1 recipe Basic Egg Pasta (p. 40), or
  ½ recipe French Noodles (p. 49)
225-g (8-oz) tinned or frozen crabmeat
3 shallots or button onions
100-g (4-oz) Ricotta cheese
2 teaspoons dried tarragon
½ teaspoon salt
1 to 2 tablespoons yogurt, cream,
  or sour cream
100-g (4-oz) butter, melted

Prepare the pasta and let it rest.

Place the crabmeat, shallots, Ricotta, tarragon, and salt in the bowl of the food processor, and process until they are well blended. Add enough yogurt or cream to make the mixture malleable.

Make and cook the ravioli by one of the methods described in the recipe for Spinach Ravioli. Place the ravioli as it's cooked in a shallow gratin pan in an oven set at 110°C (225°F), Gas ¼ to keep warm. When all the ravioli are done, pour the melted butter over them, and sprinkle with grated cheese, or serve with a delicate sauce, such as the Herbed Butter Sauce on page 74.

• In place of the crabmeat, use one 200-g (7-oz) can tuna, or 225-g (8-oz) shelled shrimps or prawns, or 225-g (8-oz) scallops.

STUFFED ZITI

Another wonderful way to use up leftover meat. This filling and the one for stuffed shells can be used interchangeably, but this one is a little simpler and less subtle. It's very good, too, made with minced beef and pork, just browned in a frying pan before it is mixed with the seasonings.

4 SERVINGS
450-g (1-lb) leftover meat, or 675-g (1½-lb)
* mixed minced beef and pork, browned*
1 clove garlic
1 onion
Few sprigs parsley
1 egg
2 tablespoons olive oil
¼ teaspoon thyme
½ teaspoon salt
Freshly ground black pepper
225-g (8-oz) large ziti
225-g (8-oz) mushrooms, sliced
15-g (½-oz) butter
350ml (12-fl oz) Light Tomato Sauce (p. 71)
Grated Parmesan cheese

Put the meat, garlic, onion, parsley, egg, olive oil, thyme, salt, and pepper in the bowl of a food processor, and process until they are well blended. If you don't mind tasting raw egg, now is the time to taste and adjust the seasoning. A lot will depend on how the meat was seasoned when it was first cooked.

Cook and drain the ziti. Using a teaspoon, fill the cooked ziti with the meat mixture. Lay them in a single layer in a shallow baking tin.

In a frying pan, sauté the mushrooms in butter until they are soft, and then spoon them over the ziti. Cover with the tomato sauce, sprinkle heavily with the grated cheese, and bake for 25 minutes in a 180°C (350°F), Gas 4 oven.

KREPLACH

There are 10 dozen ways of doing kreplach, and 10 times that number of people telling you that theirs is the traditional way. This one is idiotically simple, but the sage and chives make a nice combination of flavours. Use plenty of chives. I grow them at home, and they're usually the first thing up in the garden, so to me they taste like springtime.

6 SERVINGS
1 recipe Basic Egg Pasta (p. 40)
225-g (8-oz) minced chuck steak
1 tablespoon chopped fresh sage, or
  ½ teaspoon dried sage
1 small bunch chives, very finely chopped
3 tablespoons chopped parsley
½ teaspoon salt
¼ teaspoon Tabasco

Make the pasta dough, and while it rests mix the meat with the sage, chives, parsley, salt, and Tabasco. Roll out the dough in the pasta machine. Then, using a pastry wheel, cut it into 5-cm (2-inch) squares. Place a scant teaspoonful of filling toward one corner of each square. Moisten the edges of the square, fold one corner over another to make a triangle, and seal tightly.

Let the kreplach sit at room temperature for 30 minutes before you cook them. Drop them into salted boiling water,

154

about 8 at a time. Cover the pot and cook each batch for about 15 minutes. Remove with a slotted spoon and add more kreplach to the pot.

Add the cooked kreplach to chicken soup, or sauté them in butter or chicken fat until they are lightly browned, and serve with pot-roast beef or roast chicken.

WONTONS

Wontons can be ill-treated or well treated, and somehow they are always delicious. In San Francisco, they fry these little dumplings in hot oil for a few minutes after they are boiled. They call them 'pot stickers' because they tend to stick to the wok. If you fry them, put together a dipping sauce with soy sauce, rice vinegar, a few drops of sesame oil, and minced ginger, with some chopped coriander floating on the top.

6 SERVINGS

DOUGH:
100-g (4-oz) flour
½ teaspoon salt
¼ teaspoon baking powder
100-ml (4-fl oz) ice water

Cornflour
225-g (8-oz) minced pork
1 teaspoon very finely chopped ginger
4 teaspoons soy sauce
1 tablespoon chopped chives
½ teaspoon hot sesame oil

Put the flour, salt, baking powder, and most of the water in a bowl. Mix with a fork. Use only as much water as you need to make a mixture that is soft but not wet. Form into a ball and knead on a floured surface for 5 minutes.

Cover with a damp cloth and let rest for 30 minutes before rolling.

To make the stuffing, put the pork, ginger, soy sauce, chives, and hot sesame oil in the bowl of a food processor, and let it run until everything is well mixed.

Divide the dough in half and roll one half into a thin sheet by hand or in the machine. Dust the sheet generously with cornflour. Cut it into 7.5-cm (3-inch) squares. If you are making the squares ahead of time, you can now stack them, wrapped in aluminium foil, in the refrigerator.

To make the wontons, place a square in front of you with a point towards you. Put a heaped ¼ teaspoon filling in the centre of the square. Moisten the edges of the square and fold the point near you up to meet the point away from you, making a triangle. Press the edges together and pull the side corners towards you. Press one on top of the other. The point of the wonton that is away from you should stick up, forming a kind of bonnet for the filling.

The Chinese have an interesting method of cooking wontons. They bring a great quantity of water to a boil. Then they drop in all the dumplings, turning the heat to medium. When it boils again, they add about 300-ml (½-pt) cold water. When it comes to a boil for the third time, they add the same amount of cold water. When it comes to a boil for the fourth time, they let the wontons cook for 2 minutes, then skim them out of the cooking liquid.

TORTELLINI

Some things are so good when you buy them that they really don't repay the effort of making them. Unless you're just bound to make everything by hand and you're awfully good with pasta, tortellini may require too much handwork, especially since they are available ready-made with such high quality. But I know that there are people who won't rest until they have mastered every skill, and it is rather fun to do these tiny dumplings, if you can get the proper twist to your fingers.

They're good served cold, in a pasta salad, but I love the classic way that Alfredo Viazzi does tortellini, with a béchamel sauce studded with prosciutto and peas. Or serve them with a good tomato sauce, or with melted butter, cheese, and lots of fresh chopped parsley. About 450-g (1-lb) of sauce should be just right for this amount of tortellini.

4 TO 6 SERVINGS
1 recipe Basic Egg Pasta (p. 40)
225 g (8 oz) minced pork
2 tablespoons chopped fresh basil, or
   1 teaspoon dried basil
2 teaspoons fresh chives
1 large clove garlic, chopped
¼ teaspoon salt
½ teaspoon freshly ground black pepper

Make the pasta dough and, while it rests, mix the pork with the basil, chives, garlic, salt, and pepper in the food processor.

Roll out the dough by hand or machine until it is very thin. Using a round cutter 7.5-cm (3-inches) in diameter, cut the dough into as many circles as you can. Place a scant ½ teaspoon filling in the centre of each circle. Moisten the edges of the circle. Fold the dough over the filling and press the edges together to seal. Bend up a cuff along the curved edge. Then wrap the straight side of the tortellini around the tip of your forefinger, and seal the corners together.

Bring a pan of water to the boil. Drop in the tortellini, a few at a time. They will be done when they float to the top. Skim them out with a slotted spoon, and add more tortellini to the pan.

STEAMED MEAT PACKETS

I like to think of this as a modern lasagne. It's so much neater than lasagne, because you don't get all the sauce running into the corners of the pan, so that someone gets cheated. Serve a platter of packets at a buffet. The meat mixture is so flavourful that you might want to pat half of it into a small loaf pan and bake it at 180°C (350°F), Gas 4 for an hour. It makes very good sandwiches.

6 SERVINGS
1 recipe French Noodles (p. 49)
900-g (2-lb) good lean beef mince
450-g (1-lb) minced pork
4 cloves garlic
2 onions
1 carrot, in chunks
50-g (2-oz) soft breadcrumbs
1 teaspoon dried thyme
1 tablespoon salt
1 teaspoon freshly ground black pepper
25-g (1-oz) chopped flat-leaved parsley
2 eggs
15-g (½-oz) butter
1 recipe chèvre-tomato sauce (p. 136)
75-g (3-oz) grated Parmesan cheese

Prepare the pasta and let it rest.

Put the meats, vegetables, crumbs, and seasonings into the container of the food processor and process them until they are finely chopped. This may take as long as 30 seconds. Turn the mixture out into a bowl. Mix in the eggs. I like to use my hands for this process, but the squeamish can use a wooden spoon. To test the seasoning, melt the butter in a heavy frying pan. Form a thin patty of the meat, and fry it in the butter for about 5 minutes, until it is crusty on the outside and brown all the way through. Taste, then adjust the seasoning.

Roll the pasta in the machine or by hand, making long strips. Using a ruler as a guide, cut the strips so that they are 12.5–15-cm (5–5½-inches) wide. There are two ways to make the packets, depending on whether they will be square or triangular. The square ones are larger, contain more filling, and make a heartier serving.

For triangular packets, roll about 1 tablespoon filling lightly into a sausage. Place it to one side, about 5-cm (2-inches) up from the end of the strip of dough. Lift one corner of the strip and bring it to the opposite side, forming a triangular pocket that encloses the filling. Dip your finger into a dish of water to moisten the inner edges of the triangle and press them together. Cut the triangle free with a pastry wheel and continue up the strip.

For square packets, like oversized ravioli, put 1 heaped tablespoon of filling 7.5-cm (3-inches) up from the end of the strip of dough. This time, bring the whole end up to enclose the meat filling. Moisten the three open edges, press them together, and cut off the square with a pastry wheel. In both methods, seal the edges by pressing with the tines of a fork.

To cook, put water into the bottom part of a steamer, and bring it to a boil. Oil the top of the steamer and make a single layer of packets on it. (This is one time when it is useful to have a multi-layered Chinese steamer.) Cook the packets over boiling water for around 15 minutes. Take them out carefully and lay them in a buttered gratin dish. Coat with the sauce, sprinkle with Parmesan cheese, and bake for another 15 minutes in a 180°C (350°F), Gas 4 oven. They make an excellent luncheon dish with a serving of cold beans or asparagus vinaigrette.

FROGS' LEGS TORTELLONI

These tortelloni are the creation of chef Seppi Renngli of the Four Seasons Restaurant in New York. They have an absolutely sublime flavour, and I'm just mad about them. If you don't want to use frogs' legs, of course, you can substitute chicken, but the taste will be subtly different.

4 TO 6 SERVINGS
1 recipe Basic Egg Pasta (p. 40)
4 rashers streaky bacon
5 shallots or button onions, chopped
1 clove garlic, finely chopped
6 fresh sage leaves, or ½ teaspoon dried sage
1 celery stalk, diced
900-g (2-lb) frogs' legs
½ teaspoon salt
¼ teaspoon freshly ground black pepper
225-g (8-oz) cooked spinach
3 tablespoons Parmesan cheese
2 eggs
850-ml (1½-pt) double cream
150-g (5-oz) Gorgonzola cheese
850-ml (1½-pt) chicken stock
225-g (8-oz) mange-touts, each cut into
    3 lengthwise strips

Prepare the pasta dough and let it rest.

Cut the bacon into 2.5-cm (1-inch) pieces and cook until they are crisp. Add the shallots or onions, garlic, sage and celery. Stir over the heat for a few minutes and place the frogs' legs on top. Season with salt and pepper, cover, and cook for 20 minutes on the stove top or in a 190°C (375°F), Gas 5 oven. Set aside the frogs' legs until they are cool enough to handle. When you are able to pick the meat from the bones, add it with the spinach to the pan, and cook over high heat until all the juices have evaporated. Stir in the Parmesan cheese, taste and correct the seasoning. Put the mixture in the bowl of the food processor, process well, and let cool.

Roll out the pasta and cut into 7.5-cm (3-inch) squares. Beat the eggs and brush the dough squares with the egg wash. Place a full teaspoonful of filling in the middle of each square. Moisten the edges, fold the dough in half, and press the edges together.

Bring the cream to a boil in a heavy saucepan and simmer until it is reduced by half. Then stir in the Gorgonzola.

In a second saucepan, bring the chicken stock to a boil. Cook the tortelloni in it for 5 minutes, adding the strips of mange-touts for the last half minute of cooking. Remove the dumplings and mange-touts with a slotted spoon, and add them to the cheese-cream sauce. Shake the pan until each dumpling is well coated.

NOODLE–AUBERGINE DUMPLINGS

Don't let the length of this recipe put you off. Although there are several steps involved, they can all be done well in advance of serving. Even the final assemblage can be done in the morning of the day you're going to serve the dumplings. If you find that you have leftover stuffing, by all means save it. It will be very good the next day, lightly sautéed in a little butter and served with a salad and some crisp bread.

8 SERVINGS
1 recipe French Noodles (p. 49)
900-g (2-lb) large tomatoes
100-g (4-oz) butter
1 medium onion, sliced
Salt and freshly ground black pepper
Pinch dried red chili-pepper flakes
1 medium-sized aubergine
1½ tablespoons olive oil
40-g (1½-oz) grated Parmesan cheese
Melted butter

Mix the pasta dough and set it aside to rest.

161

Make a tomato sauce by cooking the tomatoes with the butter and onion for 2½ hours. Put them through the food processor, return to the pan, and continue to cook for another half hour, until the sauce is quite thick. Season with salt, pepper, and dried red chili-pepper.

While the sauce cooks, cut the aubergine into cubes. Put them in a bowl and cover with salted water. After 30 minutes, pour the cubes into a colander. Cover it with a plate on which you have put a weight: a tin of soup will do. Let it sit for a while so that the excess moisture drains out of the vegetable. Pat dry with paper towels, and sauté the cubes in olive oil. Add to the tomato sauce, along with half of the cheese. The filling is now all ready.

Take a little more than half the ball of dough and roll it into a very thin sheet. Cut the sheet into eight 17.5- or 20-cm (7- or 8-inch) circles. (The size of these circles will depend on the size of the ramekins in which you make the dumplings. They should be large enough to cover the bottom of the ramekin and then be gathered together over the stuffing.) Put the second half of the dough through the pasta machine and cut it into fettuccine-sized noodles.

Bring a pan of water to the boil and drop in the pasta circles, 2 at a time. Cook them for less than a minute after the water returns to the boil. Take them out with a slotted spoon, dip them into a bowl of cold water to stop the cooking, and lay them flat on a dish towel. Cook all the circles this way. Then drop the fettuccine into the boiling water. When the water returns to the boil, drain and rinse the fettuccine and stir into the tomato-aubergine mixture.

Butter 8 ramekins and set a single pasta circle into each one. Spoon in some of the filling and sprinkle with Parmesan cheese. Gather the dough around the filling, pleating it neatly as you do so. Secure it at the top with a toothpick. Brush melted butter over the top of the dough.

Bake in the upper third of a 220°C (425°F), Gas 7 oven for 8 minutes, until the dough is lightly browned. If you assemble the dumplings early in the day, cover them with a damp dish towel to keep them from drying out. When you are ready to bake them, bring them to room temperature, preheat the oven, and increase the baking time to 12 to 15 minutes.

COLD PASTA

CELLOPHANE-NOODLE SALAD
ITALIAN SAUSAGE SALAD
HERBED NOODLE SALAD
SALMON-DILL SALAD WITH PASTA SHELLS
ORZO SALAD
LEFTOVER-PASTA SALAD
SALADE NIÇOISE WITH PASTA SHELLS
MACARONI SALAD I
MACARONI SALAD II
PIQUANT SALAD
CODFISH AND BUCKWHEAT-NOODLE SALAD
(with shrimps or prawns · crabmeat ·
scallops or lobster)
COMPOSED SALAD

CELLOPHANE–NOODLE SALAD

Cellophane or transparent noodles are bouncy and fun. They are made from powdered mung beans instead of wheat flour, and the Chinese consider them a vegetable instead of a starch. They're thin and white and transparent, and you don't cook them at all. You just soak them in hot water for about 1 hour, and they're ready to use.

4 SERVINGS
100-g (4-oz) cellophane noodles
550-g (1¼-lb) diced poached chicken
150-g (5-oz) finely chopped onion or
*   spring onions*
175-g (6-oz) finely chopped celery
75-ml (3-fl oz) mayonnaise
75-ml (3-fl oz) yogurt
1 tablespoon soy sauce
½ teaspoon Tabasco
Chopped parsley

Cover the cellophane noodles with hot water and soak for 1 hour. Drain.

Combine all the ingredients in a bowl. Toss well, and serve on a bed of watercress, garnished with chopped parsley.

ITALIAN SAUSAGE SALAD

I adore all kinds of sausages; I've often said I could be happy eating nothing else. One of the simplest and best varieties is the coarsely ground Italian link sausage seasoned with garlic, basil, and anise. It's available now in most supermarkets, but if you want a real treat, make your own Italian sausage. You'll find a reliable recipe in *The New James Beard*. This salad is not a delicate nibble; it would make a wonderful picnic dish, with just a loaf of coarse bread and a really assertive red wine.

6 SERVINGS

6 Italian-style link sausages, sweet or hot
225-g (8-oz) short-cut macaroni or twists
4 green peppers, peeled and cut into strips
2 red onions, thinly sliced
350-g (12-oz) tinned haricot or cannellini
*   beans, drained*
3 hard-boiled eggs, quartered
3 tablespoons chopped flat-leaved parsley
150—175-ml (5—6-fl oz) olive oil
3 tablespoons wine vinegar
1 clove garlic, chopped
½ teaspoon salt
Freshly ground black pepper
Pinch of dried oregano

To cook the sausages, prick the skins with a fork, put them in a frying pan with water to cover, bring to a boil, reduce the heat, and poach for 1 minute. Drain off the water, slice the sausages into 1-cm (½-inch) lengths, and fry over medium heat in a dry frying pan until browned through.

Cook and drain the pasta.

Combine the sausage, peppers, onions, pasta, beans, eggs, and parsley in a bowl. In a second bowl combine the olive oil, vinegar, garlic, salt, pepper, and oregano. Beat vigorously with a fork and pour the dressing over the salad, tossing it gently as you do so. Let everything mature in the refrigerator for a few hours.

HERBED NOODLE SALAD

When I made this salad on a Saturday afternoon, it tasted sharp and oily. It went into the refrigerator until the next day, when I served it at lunch. By then, the noodles had soaked up every bit of oil and vinegar, and the taste was wonderfully improved. Be sure to allow at least 12 hours to let this happen. You'll find that this is an unusually light and pleasant salad to serve as a first course, one that doesn't ruin the appetite.

4 TO 6 SERVINGS
225-g (8-oz) buckwheat noodles or spaghetti
  (available in good health-food shops)
4 tablespoons olive oil
4 tablespoons sesame-seed oil
1 tablespoon chili sauce
3 tablespoons rice vinegar (in Japanese grocers)
40-g (1½-oz) finely chopped chives
25-g (1-oz) chopped parsley

Cook and drain the pasta. Put the freshly drained noodles into a bowl with the olive oil, so that they won't stick together as they cool. When they are cool, add the sesame oil, chili sauce, and rice vinegar. Toss well with the chives and parsley, and let stand for at least 12 hours.

SALMON-DILL SALAD WITH PASTA SHELLS

Years ago, I used to make a smoked-salmon cocktail spread very much like this using lots of shallots and cream. I think that this version, with yogurt, is even better. The pasta soaks up and holds some of the wonderful shallot and salmon flavor.

6 SERVINGS
225-g (8-oz) tiny pasta shells or twists
generous 100-g (4-oz) smoked salmon
50-ml (2-fl oz) mayonnaise
50-ml (2-fl oz) yogurt
3 tablespoons chopped shallots
Lots of finely chopped fresh dill

Cook and drain the pasta.

Cut the salmon into slivers. Then toss into a dressing made of mayonnaise, yogurt, shallots, and dill. Mix with the pasta, and refrigerate the salad for several hours to let it mellow. Taste for seasoning: you may need to add pepper, but you probably won't need any salt because of the salty taste of the salmon.

ORZO SALAD

I think orzo is just wonderful in place of rice in salads. It looks remarkably similar, but it doesn't seem to dissolve if you overcook it, as rice does. Instead of tongue, you might use an equal amount of diced chicken, turkey, or ham, two 200-g (7-oz) cans tuna fish, or 450-g (1-lb) cooked crabmeat or shrimps.

6 SERVINGS
250-g (9-oz) orzo
450-g (1-lb) diced cooked calf or ox tongue
150-g (5-oz) finely chopped spring onions
75—100-g (3—4-oz) thinly sliced fennel or celery
25-g (1-oz) finely chopped parsley
150-ml (5-fl oz) mayonnaise
50-ml (2-fl oz) yogurt
¼ teaspoon Tabasco
1 teaspoon freshly ground black pepper

Cook and drain the orzo.

Combine it with the remaining ingredients, and toss them well, using a wooden spoon or your hands. Let the salad mellow for at least 2 hours before you use it, so that the flavours have a chance to develop.

VARIATION

● Cook and cool the orzo. While it is still warm stir in, with a fork, 3 tablespoons olive oil and 50-ml (2-fl oz) wine vinegar. Toss well together. Combine cold orzo with 150-g (5-oz) sliced radishes, 75—100-g (3—4-oz) shredded cabbage, 100-g (4-oz) finely chopped stuffed olives, and 8—10 finely cut anchovy fillets. Add 150-ml (5-fl oz) olive oil, 3 tablespoons wine vinegar, and 1 or 2 crushed cloves garlic. Toss well. Serve with cold meats or fish.

LEFTOVER–PASTA SALAD

The only essentials in this recipe are the pasta and the dressing. Think of it as a pattern, one to follow when you have leftover pasta and want to do something light and bright with it. It's very good as it is, but you could empty out the refrigerator, add a little of this and that, and wind up with something even better.

4 SERVINGS
450—550-g (1—1¼-lb) leftover cooked pasta of
  any sort, except one with a soupy sauce
100-g (3½-oz) tin tuna, drained
150-g (5-oz) chopped onion
125-g (4-oz) chopped celery
75-ml (3-fl oz) yogurt
75-ml (3-fl oz) mayonnaise
1 tablespoon Dijon mustard
1 tablespoon chopped fresh dill

If there is sauce clinging to the pasta, rinse it in a colander under lots of cold water. Shake it dry, and put it in a bowl with the tuna, onion, and celery.

In a small bowl beat together the yogurt, mayonnaise, mustard, and dill. Then toss the dressing with the pasta, and let the mixture rest for at least 30 minutes at room temperature before you serve it.

VARIATION

- If you have cold beef or veal or chicken add 450-g (1-lb) diced (cooked boiled beef is especially good), plus 125-g (4-oz) finely chopped celery, 175-g (6-oz) chopped spring onions, and 175-g (6-oz) coarsely shredded carrots. Add garlic-flavoured vinaigrette to taste. Toss the salad and arrange in a bowl. Garnish with freshly sliced dill cucumber and quartered hard-boiled eggs.

SALADE NIÇOISE WITH PASTA SHELLS

Salade Niçoise must have tuna, tomato, olives, onions and potatoes — but how they are put together is nobody's business but your own. This time, we used pasta shells instead of the usual potatoes, which seems a very pleasant way to change the formula.

2 SERVINGS
125-g (4-oz) small shells or other pasta
50-ml (2-fl oz) olive oil
3 tablespoons tarragon vinegar
1 large clove garlic, chopped
4 heads chicory, quartered
1 tin anchovies
4 medium tomatoes, peeled and cut in wedges
100-g (3½-oz) tin tuna
125—150-g (4—5-oz) black olives
3 hard-boiled eggs, quartered
1 red onion, cut in rings
1 tablespoon capers

VINAIGRETTE:
175-ml (6-fl oz) olive oil
3 tablespoons white wine vinegar
25-g (1-oz) coarsely chopped basil leaves
2 teaspoons Worcestershire sauce
1 teaspoon freshly ground black pepper

Cook and drain the pasta. Combine the pasta shells with the olive oil, tarragon vinegar, and garlic. Cover, and marinate for 2 to 3 hours.

Place the marinated pasta in the centre of an oval platter, with the chicory at either end. Put the anchovies alongside the chicory, and arrange the tomatoes, tuna, olives, eggs, and onion rings attractively around the pasta. Sprinkle capers over everything.

Blend the ingredients for the vinaigrette and pour over the salad just before you serve it, or pass the sauce separately in a bowl.

MACARONI SALAD I

Macaroni salad is standard picnic fare in much of America. You can do it with endless variations, adding mustard, peppers, onions, or chives. But for the greatest improvement, try making it with a home-made mayonnaise. Then you get a fresh taste, and avoid the awful three-days-old taste that you sometimes get from delicatessen macaroni salad.

6 SERVINGS
1 egg
2 egg yolks
1 tablespoon lemon juice or vinegar
1 teaspoon salt
¼ teaspoon freshly ground black pepper
350-ml (12-fl oz) olive oil, or half olive
   and half peanut oil
175-g (6-oz) macaroni
2 teaspoons Dijon mustard
2 cloves garlic, chopped
2 medium onions, chopped
300-g (10-oz) chopped celery
3 red peppers, peeled, and sliced
3 hard-boiled eggs, sliced
15-g (½-oz) chopped parsley

Make the mayonnaise in the food processor. (To make it by hand or in the blender, you will have to adjust the proportions.) With the metal blade in place, add the egg and egg yolks, lemon juice, salt, and pepper. Process until they are blended, about 3 seconds. Continue processing as you slowly pour the oil through the feeding tube. Taste to see if it needs more vinegar, salt, or pepper. This recipe makes about 425-ml (¾-pt) mayonnaise. Measure out 225-ml (8-fl oz) for the salad, and put the rest in a container, cover, and store in the refrigerator. It will be good for a week to 10 days.

Cook and drain the pasta.

Mix the mayonnaise and mustard in a large bowl. Toss in all the other ingredients, blend with the dressing, and refrigerate until ready to serve.

MACARONI SALAD II

A very different macaroni salad, and a recipe large enough to take with you to a picnic. It's astonishing how the flavours dull out when the dish is chilled. The vinaigrette will seem quite tangy when it is first mixed, but when it is given a few hours to mellow, it will become blunted.

8 SERVINGS
450-g (1-lb) short-cut macaroni
4 or 5 celery stalks, thinly sliced
16 spring onions, thinly sliced
2 medium carrots, shredded
2 long, preserved green chili peppers,
    peeled and chopped
50-g (2-oz) chopped parsley
125-ml (4-fl oz) olive oil, or more if needed
3 tablespoons vinegar
1 tablespoon Dijon mustard
1 teaspoon salt
½ teaspoon freshly ground black pepper

Cook and drain the pasta. Toss the cooked macaroni with the vegetables. Make a vinaigrette by beating together the oil, vinegar, mustard, salt, and pepper, and mix into the salad. Chill before serving.

PIQUANT SALAD

This is a substantial salad to serve at a summer luncheon with slices of cold ham or roast pork.

4 TO 6 SERVINGS
225-g (8-oz) pasta elbows, shells, or twists
2 tablespoons finely chopped onion
8 streaky bacon rashers, cooked, drained,
   and crumbled
75-ml (3-fl oz) mayonnaise
100-ml (4-fl oz) olive oil
2 tablespoons wine vinegar
2 tablespoons tomato ketchup
1 teaspoon capers
½ teaspoon salt
Freshly ground black pepper
Tomatoes and hard-boiled eggs, for garnish

Cook and drain the pasta.

In a salad bowl, mix the drained pasta with the onion, bacon, and mayonnaise. In a screw-top jar, combine the olive oil, vinegar, ketchup, capers, salt, and pepper, and shake it vigorously. Pour this over the pasta mixture and mix it well: hands do a very good job here. Surround it with a border of alternating tomato wedges and hard-boiled egg quarters.

CODFISH AND BUCKWHEAT–NOODLE SALAD

I must have Portuguese blood in me, because I love codfish so. But then, dried cod dishes are found all over the world. This salad is a steal from one that is made in central Europe, where they include lots of potatoes. I've just substituted chewy buckwheat noodles for the potatoes.

> 900-g (2-lb) dried salted codfish (available in
>   Continental grocers)
> 450-g (1-lb) buckwheat noodles or spaghetti
> 175-ml (6-fl oz) peanut oil
> 3 tablespoons vinegar
> 1 tablespoon Dijon mustard
> 3 tablespoons soy sauce
> 2 large cloves garlic, finely chopped
> 12 shallots, chopped, or about 150-g (5-oz)
>   chopped onion
> 25-g (1-oz) chopped parsley

The night before you plan to cook the fish, put it to soak in cold water. Change the water several times to soften the fillets and remove the salt. When you are ready to cook the fish, drain it, put it in a saucepan, and cover it with fresh water. Bring to a boil and simmer 15 minutes, or until tender. Drain, and set aside.

Cook and drain the noodles.

Make a dressing of the oil, vinegar, mustard, soy sauce, garlic, and shallots or onions. Break the fish apart with a fork or your fingers. Mix it with the noodles, the vinaigrette, and the chopped parsley. Serve on a bed of salad greens (lettuce, watercress, fresh spinach etc), garnished with lemon wedges and sprigs of parsley.

VARIATION
- Instead of the codfish, use 450-g (1-lb) shrimps, prawns, crabmeat, or scallops, or the equivalent amount of lobster

meat. If you use fresh fish, you will not, of course, soak it before you cook it, and will probably cut down the cooking time, depending on the thickness of the fish.

COMPOSED SALAD

Composed salads are so much fun. You do a still life, a great picture on a platter, and then everyone eats what he wants. This, by the way, is the answer to people who say that noodles are fattening. The only calories worth counting in this composed salad are in the olive oil and the duck skin. I used Chinese cellophane or transparent noodles, made of mung-bean flour.

8 SERVINGS
75-g (3-oz) cellophane noodles
1.8-kg (4-lb) mushrooms
3 shallots or button onions, finely chopped
100-ml (4-fl oz) olive oil
50-ml (2-fl oz) wine vinegar
1 tablespoon Dijon mustard
1 teaspoon salt
1 teaspoon freshly ground black pepper
1 duck breast, cooked and skinned
2 to 3 heads Webb's Wonderful lettuce
2 heads Cos lettuce
2 bunches spring onions, shredded
4—6 beetroots, cooked, peeled, and sliced
100-g (4-oz) mange-touts

VINAIGRETTE:
1 teaspoon coarse salt
½ teaspoon freshly ground black pepper
1 teaspoon Dijon mustard
2 tablespoons wine vinegar
100-ml (4-fl oz) fruity olive oil
Chopped parsley

Begin by preparing the transparent noodles. These must be soaked before they are cooked. Because they overcook in no time at all, we've had to work out a way to keep them from melting into jelly. Cover the noodles with cold water and let them soak for an hour. Drain them, return them to the bowl, cover with boiling water, and let them cool in the water for 30 minutes. Drain and set aside.

Wipe the mushrooms with damp paper towels. Remove the stems, and put them aside to use in a soup or stew. Put the caps in a bowl with the shallots or onions, olive oil, vinegar, mustard, salt, and pepper. Mix well, cover, and marinate for at least 1 hour.

Remove the duck skin from the meat, and slice both skin and meat into thin strips. Put the meat aside and fry the strips of skin in very hot oil in a frying pan until they are crisp. Set the pieces aside to drain on a paper towel.

Now arrange the lettuce leaves decoratively on a large platter. On them, arrange the drained marinated mushrooms, the noodles, spring onions, beetroots, duck breast, and peas. The whole point of a composed salad is its composition, so use all your skill in the arrangement.

You can prepare the salad ahead to this point. Just before you serve it, mix a vinaigrette of salt, pepper, Dijon mustard, vinegar, and oil. Spoon it over the salad, and garnish with strips of crisp duck skin and with chopped parsley.

STORE CUPBOARD SAUCES

When I was testing the pasta recipes for this book I very often found myself with an embarrassment of riches at lunchtime. The simplest solution was to put the hot cooked noodles in a bowl, drop in a nugget of unsalted butter, and toss it with whatever cheese I had in the refrigerator.

But there were other solutions that were nearly as simple, and were often more delicious than prepared, long-cooked sauces. For example, I might melt the butter into the pasta and then simply grind a good deal of coarsely cracked peppercorns over it. Almost any fresh herb melted in butter was good. Chopped parsley, butter, and minced garlic made a sublime sauce. And another lunch of pasta, herbs, and butter became the inspiration for the tarragon-shallot-butter sauce on page 74.

The point is that you need never be at a loss for something good to eat if you have some pasta and the resources of an ordinary kitchen. I remember one memorable meal that Marion Cunningham and I put together at La Costa, where we were giving a series of cooking demonstrations. We didn't want to eat at the spa, and we were too tired to go out to dinner. We hung around until it got late, and then we tore down to the little local grocery shop and found, to our dismay, that it was closed. Back to our demonstration kitchen we went and surveyed what we had on hand. We found a package of imported spaghettini and a couple of cans of *salsa*, the spicy onion, pepper, and green tomato sauce that is used in Mexican cooking. We cooked the pasta, dumped the *salsa*, cold, on the steaming hot spaghettini, tossed it all together, and to this day Marion claims that it's the best pasta dish she's ever had.

I've never been the sort who knew on Monday what he wanted to eat on Tuesday. Or, for that matter, who knew at three what he wanted for supper at eight. That's why I've found pasta such a resource for spontaneous, last-minute meals.

It's endless, for example, what you can do with pasta and fresh vegetables. (Even cabbage, as on page 82; even beans, as on page 83.) I might sauté broccoli florets in olive oil with garlic and pour it over shells. Stir-fry broccoli stems in peanut oil, season them with ginger and soy sauce, and serve them on a bed of cellophane noodles. Or steam the broccoli, add it to canned tomato sauce with a little cream and a good dash of Tabasco, and serve it over penne.

Here, then, is a collection of ideas that I hardly think of as recipes, but rather as last-minute inspirations for using pasta. Each one began with a quick review of what I had on hand that day in the cupboard or in the refrigerator. Each one made a gratifying meal. But then, of course, I love pasta.

LEMON JUICE AND PEPPER

I haven't eaten baked potatoes with butter or salt for years. Instead, I squeeze on some lemon juice and then add a lot of freshly ground black pepper. If you don't want to have any oil with your pasta, there's no reason you can't treat it similarly.

GARLIC AND OIL

Nobody ever has to dine badly if he has olive oil, garlic, and fresh pepper. Heat 100-ml (4-fl oz) oil in a saucepan with 4 cloves finely chopped garlic. When the garlic is soft, but not brown, pour the scented oil over 225-g (8-oz) of freshly cooked pasta, and grind lots of fresh pepper on top.

PARSLEY AND CHEESE

Melt 100-g (4-oz) butter with a clove of garlic. Then put a bunch of parsley into the bowl of the processor with a big chunk of cheese, and process well. Put some freshly drained pasta into the butter and immediately stir in the parsley and cheese, which should melt beautifully into the butter.

PASTA AND PEPPERS

One day I found myself ready for lunch with nothing promising on hand except some fresh pasta and a bowl in the refrigerator full of roasted green peppers in a vinaigrette sauce. I put the peppers and sauce in the processor and served the purée over the hot pasta. But I could also have sliced the peppers into slivers, perhaps added some spring onions, and poured that with the vinaigrette over the pasta.

YOGURT SAUCE

It's not at all traditional, but I've taken a liking to yogurt served with pasta. I make a luncheon salad by mixing cooked noodles with 175—225-ml (6—8-fl oz) yogurt into which I stir about 15-g (½-oz) chopped parsley, 2 tablespoons chopped chives, and some tarragon leaves, then let it all cool to room temperature.

COTTAGE CHEESE

A friend tells me that the happiest meals of his childhood were in his German grandmother's kitchen, where he watched her cut out wide egg noodles, and then was served a bowl of the freshly cooked noodles mixed with cold cottage cheese sprinkled with cinnamon-sugar.

CUCUMBER SALAD

I can see an icy-cold dish of cucumbers and onion in vinegar or yogurt tossed with hot pasta.

DUXELLES

This delicious mushroom paste is used in stuffings, omelettes, crêpes, or simply spread on thin toast for an appetiser. I don't suggest that you make it up for a pasta sauce, but if you have some duxelles in the refrigerator, you could well use it for an instant sauce. For the recipe, see *The New James Beard*, page 535. To use it as a sauce for pasta, spoon off about 100-g (4-oz) of the paste. Warm it in a heavy pan and thin it with some cream until it is the proper consistency.

QUICK CREAM AND TOMATO SAUCE

I can't deny that this is best when it's made with home-made tomato sauce. But, on the other hand, if you find yourself with a tin or jar of commercially made tomato sauce (*not* ketchup), here's a way to turn it into something special. Heat the tomato sauce with the juice of half an orange, a dash of Tabasco, and about 50-ml (2-fl oz) cream. Warm through and pour over hot pasta.

HAM AND PEAS

Very simple. Pour 225-ml (8-fl oz) double cream into a saucepan. Let it cook down and thicken slightly, and add some peas and bits of ham. Pour over hot pasta and sprinkle on quite a lot of grated cheese.

ANCHOVY SAUCE

Everyone has a tin of anchovies in his cupboard. Drain the oil into a measuring jug, and add enough olive oil to make it up to 150-ml (¼-pt). Pour the oil into a saucepan with 2 cloves chopped garlic and the anchovies. Heat them all with 2 tablespoons hot water. Pour over the pasta and sprinkle with lots of chopped parsley.

MUSHROOM SAUCE

What could be better? Sauté a lot of sliced mushrooms in butter with just a hint of garlic. Toss with the pasta and add lots of chopped chives.

RAISIN AND PINE KERNEL SAUCE

Made in minutes, if you have pine kernels on hand. If you don't, don't despair: almonds will do in a pinch. Heat 175-ml

(6-fl oz) olive oil with 4 cloves garlic, chopped fine. Add 50-g (2-oz) nuts and 75-g (3-oz) raisins, and heat through. Serve over pasta, sprinkled with lots of fresh pepper and chopped parsley.

QUICK TUNA SAUCE

Warm 100-ml (4-fl oz) olive oil with a clove of garlic. Dump in a 200-g (7-oz) tin of tuna, and break it up with a fork. Then add a lot of chopped parsley, heat through, and pour over the pasta. Add a few chopped black olives, if you have them.

SMOKED SALMON AND SCOTCH

I used to make this years ago. Warm some double cream with a good knob of butter. When it has cooked down a little, pour in a splash of Scotch whisky. Let it heat through and pour over the noodles. Then toss in as much smoked salmon, cut into shreds, as you have. If you don't have smoked salmon, do it with kipper fillets or other smoked fish.

OLIVES

Take some of the lovely black Greek olives, mix them with a little garlic and olive oil and spring onions, and pour them over pasta. Green olives will do, too.

OYSTERS

Take freshly opened oysters, toss them briefly with hot melted butter and pour them into a bowl of pasta. The heat from the noodles will continue to cook them. Serve with lemon wedges.

TINNED TOMATO SAUCE

In the best of all possible worlds all tomato sauce would be freshly made. But this is not the best of all possible worlds, and sometimes that extra 20 minutes is just too long to spend on preparing dinner. That's why it's wise to have some tinned tomato sauce in your store cupboard. (Small tins and jars are available in Italian and other Continental grocers.)

These sauces are as useful as tinned tomatoes. Some are abysmally bad, while others are better, frankly, than fresh sauces that some people would make. The packing companies are often able to get better tomatoes than we do. And there are many small companies around the country that package really high-quality sauces.

As for the bad ones, you can always dress them up. Take a canned sauce as a starting point. Then add some browned chopped meat; or leftover meat and gravy; or a can of tuna and some parsley. Put in some mushrooms sautéed in butter. Pour in some cream: that helps a lot. Add herbs. Keep on tasting. Use your imagination.

DESSERTS

MACARONI PUDDING
NOODLE PUDDING

MACARONI PUDDING

Pasta for dessert? What a wicked thought! Now that we have had our noodles in soup, as appetisers, with meat and fish and eggs and salad, let's pay a final tribute to excess and have a wonderful macaroni pudding. This is a very old English recipe that probably dates at least from the eighteenth century. And you can trust the English when it comes to sweets — it's awfully good.

> 4 SERVINGS
> *125—150-g (4—5-oz) short-cut macaroni*
> *75-g (3-oz) raisins*
> *50-ml (2-fl oz) rum*
> *450-ml (16-fl oz) milk*
> *4 egg yolks*
> *100-g (3½-oz) caster sugar*
> *1 teaspoon vanilla or almond essence*

Cook and drain the pasta.

Cover the raisins with rum and set them aside to soak.

Put the milk in a heavy saucepan over medium-high heat. When it is nearly scalded, just before tiny bubbles appear around the edge of the pan, begin to beat the egg yolks and sugar in the electric mixer. Keep the mixer going while you pour in the hot milk. Add the vanilla, and pour into a baking dish. Stir in the macaroni and the drained raisins, and bake in a 180°C (350°F), Gas 4 oven for 45 minutes. The pudding will continue to set as it cools, but it is wonderful hot, too.

NOODLE PUDDING

This famous Jewish speciality looks and tastes like a dessert. It is usually served in a kosher meal with the main course as a sweet starch, something on the order of candied sweet potatoes. I've saved it for the end of the book because I really enjoy it more as a dessert.

I've had two kinds of noodle pudding. One is made with cottage cheese and sour cream and goes with 'dairy' meals, and the other is made with fruit and goes with meat meals. When I adapted the recipe, I used butter in place of the traditional vegetable oil or margarine, and I think it adds to the quality.

4 TO 6 SERVINGS
225-g (8-oz) wide noodles
4 eggs, lightly beaten
scant 50-g (2-oz) caster sugar
¼ teaspoon ground ginger
100-g (4-oz) butter, melted
1 teaspoon salt
2 cooking apples, peeled and diced
50-g (2-oz) raisins
75-g (3-oz) dried apricots, cut in sixths
½ teaspoon powdered cinnamon mixed with
    2 teaspoons sugar

Cook and drain the noodles.

Mix them with everything but the cinnamon-sugar. Pour the mixture into a buttered 1.7-litre (3-pt) baking dish, sprinkle the top with the cinnamon-sugar, dot with more butter, and bake at 180°C (350°F), Gas 4 for 40 minutes.

PASTA VARIETIES

This book was originally written for American readers, and many pasta names in the book may not be familiar to British cooks. But then, many pastas have different names, shapes, uses, depending on the country — or region even — of origin. The following listing should help, but the best thing to do is to go to a Continental or Oriental grocer or supermarket and just explore.

Acine de pepe, see *Pastina*

Angel's hair, *Capelli d' angelo*: The thinnest variety of ribbon pasta. Available dried, in nests.

Bows or Butterflies, *Farfalli*: Pasta in various sizes which looks like a bow tie or (less) a butterfly. Also *farfallini*.

Buckwheat noodles or spaghetti: Occasionally available in dried form in health-food shops. The Japanese *soba* noodle is made from golden buckwheat, and these may be obtained in Japanese grocers.

Butterflies, see Bows

Cellophane or Transparent noodles: Vermicelli-like noodles from China and Japan, made from mung-bean paste, and occasionally from pea starch or wheat.

Egg noodles: Noodles — from the German word for dumplings, *nudeln* — are made from eggs (most Italian pasta isn't). They are available, mostly dried, but sometimes fresh, coming from America, Central Europe or China. In China they are known as *mein* or *mee*, and come like loosely tangled rectangles or balls of wool in various thicknesses.

Elbow macaroni: The American name for *tubetti lunghi*, a macaroni in many variations of short curved tubes.

Fettucine: The Roman ribbon pasta, narrower than *tagliatelle*.

Funghini, see *Pastina*

Gnocchi: Small dumplings or lumps of pasta. Available dried, made from durum wheat, potatoes or semolina.

Lasagne: The widest pasta. Available in strips or squares, fresh or dried, smooth or ridged, or with ruffled edges. Made from durum wheat, whole-wheat, or with spinach

— giving it the name *lasagne verdi*.

Linguine: Small tongues. Short lengths of oval-section macaroni.

Maccheroni, macaroni: Generic name for dried pasta, but commonly used to describe hollow spaghetti. Available in all thicknesses from thinnest spaghetti to thickest *cannelloni*, in all lengths, and made from durum or whole-wheat flour.

Mung-bean noodles, see Cellophane noodles

Orzo: a rice-like *pastina*, available dried in different sizes.

Pastina: Small dried pasta of any shape for cooking *in brodo*, in soup or stock. These include *lunache, conchigliette, farfallini, ditalini, ruotini, gnocchetti, pennette, perline, puntine, sedani, stelle, stellini, trinate, orzo, tubetti, funghini, acine de pepe, anellini*.

Penne: Smooth or ribbed macaroni cut diagonally like a pen nib or quill at the ends. Also *pennette, pennine, pennone*.

Ravioli: The best known pasta dumpling, usually rectangular with a ruffled edge. Available freshly made or dried.

Rice noodles: These are available, dried, in Chinese supermarkets, and are thickish (known as rice sticks) or very thin (rice vermicelli).

Shells, Sea shells, *Conchiglie*: Dried pasta shaped like cockle shells, available in several sizes.

Spaghetti: Means little strings (and known as *vermicelli* in Southern Italy). Long rounded pasta, available in various thicknesses and lengths, fresh or dried, made from durum wheat, whole-wheat or buckwheat.

Tagliatelle: From *tagliare*, to cut, a speciality of Bologna. Ribbon pasta or egg noodles, a little wider than the Roman *fettucine*. Available dried or fresh, made from durum wheat, whole-wheat, or with spinach (*verdi*). Also *tagliarini, taglioletti, tagliolini*.

Tortellini: Twists of stuffed egg pasta that look like a navel. Available fresh or dried, made from durum wheat or spinach.

Tortelloni: A stuffed pasta, slightly larger than ravioli. Available fresh.

Trenette: A flat dried noodle. From Genoa, a narrower and thicker version of *tagliatelle*.

Tubetti, see *Pastina*

Twists, *Fusilli*: Spaghetti made in spiral shape, like a corkscrew or spring. Similar shapes are *cavatappi* and *spirale*.

Udon noodles: Very narrow, ribbon-like white wheat noodles from Japan. Sold in Japanese grocer's shops, dried, or wet-packed along with a container of soup-base.

Whole-wheat pasta: Available in many shapes and sizes, fresh or dried, from supermarkets, health-food and speciality shops.

Wheels, *Ruoti*: Dried pasta in the shape of a wagon wheel with spokes, available in several sizes. Also known as *Tatelle*.

Ziti: Short-cut macaroni, fatter than *tubetti lunghi*. Also *zitoni*, large, *mezze ziti*, average.

SUPPLIERS

Most delicatessens and general food shops now have a variety of pasta on sale, but for the more unusual types you may have to visit a specialist shop. Here are just a few names to help you.

London
Fratelli Camisa
1a Berwick Street, W1

I. Camisa and Son
61 Old Compton Street, W1

Gastronomia Italia
8 Upper Tachbrooke Street, SW1

G.M. Gazzano & Son
167—168 Farringdon Road, EC1

Lina Stores
18 Brewer Street, W1

Luigi's
60 New King's Road, SW6
349 Fulham Road, SW10

G. Parmigiani Figlio
36a Old Compton Street, W1

Bristol
Carmelo Licata & Son
36 Picton Street

Cambridge
P. Balzano & Sons
26 Ainsworth Street

Cardiff
Berni's
57 Wellfield Road

Edinburgh
Valvona and Crolla Ltd
19 Elm Row

Glasgow
Fazzi Brothers
232 Clyde Street

Manchester
Italian Village
Lower Ground Floor, Royal Exchange

The above are all Italian specialists. For German noodles try the German Food Centre, 44 Knightsbridge, London SW1. Dried Chinese noodles are now widely available, especially in all Oriental groceries.

INDEX

198

201